COMPUTER FUN FOR EVERYONE

D1501771

Great Things to Do and Make with Any Computer

Elin Kordahl Saltveit
with Mark Saltveit

John Wiley & Sons, Inc.

New York   Chichester   Weinheim   Brisbane   Singapore   Toronto

SOMERSET COUNTY LIBRARY
BRIDGEWATER, N. J. 08807

To sweet Anna, and to my parents for a lifetime of encouragement

ACKNOWLEDGMENTS

Thanks to my students and colleagues at Schools of the Sacred Heart (San Francisco), the James P. Timilty School (Boston Public Schools), and Sleepy Hollow Elementary School (Orinda, CA Public Schools) for your experimentation and support. Recognition to the following organizations for giving me a platform to share and incubate ideas: NECC (National Education Computing Conference), CUE (Computer Using Educators), SFCUE, BAISnet (Bay Area Independent Schools Network), UC Berkeley, Lesley College, and the University of San Francisco. Appreciation to the following folks for fun collaboration over the years: Mary, Janet, Jamie, Lori, Carol, Marilyn, Tracy, Caroline, Hoover, Jason, and Joanne. Gratitude to John Wright for helping me to share these ideas and to Kate (and folks at John Wiley & Sons) for your terrific editing. "Bickle" to the Prague Kordahls for your generous hospitality and interest. Without my parents' extraordinary support I would have never found the time to write this.

This book is printed on acid-free paper. ∞

Copyright © 1998 by Elin Kordahl Saltveit. All rights reserved.

Published by John Wiley & Sons, Inc.

Design and production by Navta Associates, Inc.

Published simultaneously in Canada

KidPix Stamps from Kidpix © 1994, 1996 Broderbund Software, Inc.
Screen shot on p. 84 copyright The European Internet Network, Inc. www.einnetworks.com
Screen shots from ClarisWorks 4.0 courtesy of Apple Computer, Inc. Used with permission.
Screen shots from Internet Explorer reprinted by permission from Microsoft Corporation.
Eudora is a registered trademark of QUALCOMM Incorporated.

No part of this publication may be reproduced, stored in a retrieval system or transmitted in any form or by any means, electronic, mechanical, photocopying, recording, scanning or otherwise, except as permitted under Sections 107 or 108 of the 1976 United States Copyright Act, without either the prior written permission of the Publisher, or authorization through payment of the appropriate per-copy fee to the Copyright Clearance Center, 222 Rosewood Drive, Danvers, MA 01923, (508) 750-8400, fax (508) 750-4744. Requests to the Publisher for permission should be addressed to the Permissions Department, John Wiley & Sons, Inc., 605 Third Avenue, New York, NY 10158-0012, (212) 850-6011, fax (212) 850-6008, E-Mail: PERMREQ @ WILEY.COM.

The publisher and the author have made every reasonable effort to ensure that the experiments and activities in this book are safe when conducted as instructed but assume no responsibility for any damage caused or sustained while performing the experiments or activities in the book. Parents, guardians, and/or teachers should supervise young readers who undertake the experiments and activities in this book.

Library of Congress Cataloging-in-Publication Data:

Saltveit, Elin Kordahl.
     Computer fun for everyone : great things to do and make with any computer / Elin Kordahl Saltveit.
        p.   cm.
     Includes index.
     Summary: Presents a variety of projects using computers to create such things as coloring books, comic books, stationery, an email diary, mazes, party invitations, rebuses, and more.
     ISBN 0-471-24450-3 (pbk. : alk. paper)
     1. Computer art—juvenile literature.   2. Handicraft—Data processing—Juvenile literature.
[1. Handicraft—Data processing.   2. Computer art.]   I. Title
TT869.5.S25   1998
745.5--dc21   97-49026

Printed in the United States of America

10 9 8 7 6 5 4 3 2 1

Contents

Letter to Parents

Dear Parents,

You already know that kids love computers and are always looking for new ways to use them. It might even seem that your children know computers inside and out, but they don't. In my twelve years teaching with computers, I've often seen kids start the school year saying, "I know how to do this. I know the program already." Of course, they don't really. They know a few commands, but not *why* they should use the program or what to do with it. This book gives parents and kids many ways to creatively explore computers together.

It would be easy to write a book full of fun and meaningless things to do on computers (and there is a place for that!). But there are plenty of fun *and* educational things to be done first. Kids like making worthwhile projects, and they see through empty ones. If a project seems "stupid," your child will get bored and bug you for something else to do.

Skeptics will ask, "Why do we need a computer to do these projects?" Computers aren't absolutely necessary for several of these projects, but using computers to create them is easier and more fun for your child, and he or she will practice and learn useful computer skills by doing these projects. Here are just some of the general advantages to using computers (individual projects have specific reasons, too, of course):

• The ability to make minor changes without having to start from scratch.

• Easy backups, so that lost work isn't devastating.

• Printing multiple copies without a photocopy machine.

• A fun (and educational) alternative to endless TV-watching.

• It's easy to share and transmit work. You can send copies of projects to friends, parents, and grandparents on computer disk or via E-mail, no matter how far away they live.

• Computers make it easy for children to combine several of these projects into a book or portfolio that they can keep, show to friends, send to relatives, and so forth.

Of course, by doing these projects, your child is either learning or reinforcing important computer skills: using draw tools, manipulating graphics, editing their work, creating page layout, copying and pasting, formatting text, centering and aligning, sending and receiving E-mail, saving files, practicing keyboard familiarity, learning special keyboard tricks, multitasking between programs, printing, and so on. It's silly to try to teach computer skills directly, because the details change so rapidly, but these concepts and general comfort with computers will help your child for a lifetime.

These fun, anytime activities teach a lot of different things, from computer skills (using the mouse, copying and pasting, etc.) to the most important fundamentals, reading and writing.

Each project includes step-by-step instructions, as well as variations.

Even though your children can work through these projects alone, I hope you will do them together whenever possible. Help them get started and be sure to review (and admire) their finished work. They love your attention and will stay interested longer when they know you care. You can even use these projects to get chores done, such as creating a letterhead so they can thank their grandparents for gifts.

Have fun with your kids. Learn from each other. And remember—the computer is only a tool, like a pencil or ruler. You and your child really learn from each other.

Not only will you have fun at the computer together, but you may find yourself creating new projects as you go. I would love to hear about them.

You or your children can write me at P.O. Box 471258, San Francisco CA 94147 with your ideas, corrections, and other information. I'll post the best ideas on my Web site, which is at http://www.realchange.org/compideas.

If I use the idea in a future book, you'll get an autographed copy. Or E-mail me (elin@realchange.org).

How This Book Works

This book has dozens of computer projects that you can do by yourself or with your parents. For each project, I will tell you these important facts:

Challenge Level

The projects are ranked from one disk (easiest) to three disks (most difficult) based on the computer skills involved.

Things You'll Need

This section lists any materials you will need for the project in addition to the basics: computer, printer, disks, and some word-processing and/or graphics software (for example, household items like scissors and tape, and anything special, such as egg cartons or paint).

For the computer, it doesn't matter whether you have a Macintosh or a PC-compatible machine (running Windows, Windows 95, or DOS), or even an older computer such as an Amiga or Apple II. These projects are designed around the basic things that all computers do, not commands or features specific to any program or machine.

For most projects, you will need a printer, too. (If you don't have a printer, you might be able to print your files at school or at a friend's house, or maybe one of your parents can print it at work for you.)

You also need to have the right kind of software to do each project—not any one particular program, but the right *type* of program. These types are discussed beginning on page vii.

And you should always back up your files on a floppy disk or Zip disk as well as the hard drive of your computer. If you only have one copy, then it is disastrous if you accidentally delete or damage your file. So make sure you have some kind of disk you can save extra copies of your files on.

What You Do

I have tried to list everything you have to do as specifically and clearly as possible, but it would be silly to explain every little step. This book assumes that you know the basics about computers in general and your software in particular—how to turn on the computer and start the program, open and save files, print a document, and so on.

If you don't understand how to do something, the first thing to do, of course, is to ask your parents. If they are busy, you can ask your brother or sister, or a friend, or a teacher. If none of these work, you can send me E-mail at elin@realchange.org, but it might take a while for me to write back, because I get a *lot* of E-mail.

Computer commands are printed in CAPITAL LETTERS, so they are easy to see. Remember to save your work frequently as you go through each project so that you don't lose any of your hard work. To be extra-safe, you should save each file on your computer's hard drive, and also on a floppy disk when you are done.

Sometimes you do a project in different ways depending on what kind of software you have. In that case, I list different directions for each kind of program.

Things to Watch Out For

If there is anything especially tricky about a project, or a mistake that's easy to make, I warn you about it in this section.

Variations

Each project has a basic idea, but sometimes you can use that idea in different ways. For example, you can draw your own comic book on your computer at home. But if you're going on a long car vacation and you can't bring your computer along, one variation shows you how to print blank pages for your comic so you can draw it with a pencil in the car. I describe these other ideas in the Variations section, but I won't repeat all the steps because they are basically the same as for the main project.

Software You Can Use

These projects use the basic functions most common to computers—word processing and graphics. These functions will be around for a long time, and won't change dramatically (though they will probably get easier to do). None of these projects requires one particular program.

However, there are several broad categories of programs, and it's important for you to know which ones you have. For most projects, any of these programs will work. If the project needs something more specific, I say so.

Five years from now, the popular programs will probably be different, but the following categories will be the same.

WORD-PROCESSING PROGRAMS WITH GRAPHICS

Most recent word processors allow you to copy, paste, and sometimes even draw graphic images in your documents. This is very convenient, because it means you don't have to buy and learn a separate graphics program, or switch between programs while working.

If you have one of these programs, you can use it for almost all of these projects. You can do all of your writing and also make drawings in the same document.

Examples include Microsoft Word, WordPerfect for Windows or Macintosh, Ami Pro and Word Pro, and all-around programs such as Microsoft Works or ClarisWorks.

WordPad, which comes free with Windows 95, lets you paste graphics into documents but not actually create them. You can draw the programs in the Paint program, also free with Windows 95, copy them, and paste them into WordPad.

These programs will also change and upgrade in future years. Not only will these projects still work, but working with graphics and word processing together is going to get even easier.

ANY WORD PROCESSOR

For projects that don't include any graphics, you can use any word processor, including all programs described above and the small word processors that come free with your computer, such as NotePad, WordPad, SimpleText, MacWrite, and Edit.

If that is the only software you have, you can still do many of these projects—almost all of the Writing projects, and many of the Top Secret Codes.

Older DOS and Apple II word processors (such as WordPerfect 5.1 for DOS, Multimate, and WordStar) are harder to use, however. If you have one of these programs, you may have to get more help from your parents.

GRAPHICS PROGRAMS

At least half of these projects include drawing, so you will need some kind of graphics program to do them. These programs usually have a graphics toolbar with different drawing tools, like a pencil, an eraser, a paint can, and so on. You click on the tool, then draw (or erase) with it.

KidPix is a fun graphics program specifically designed for kids. The buttons are bigger and easier to click, the program makes lots of funny noises, you can stamp ready-made pictures anywhere you like, and you can blow it all up if you don't like the results.

We use KidPix at my school and the kids love it, but you can make the same drawings with any drawing/graphics program out there. Generally speaking, the simpler the program the better. Paintbrush (for Windows 3.1) and Paint (for Windows 95) are free programs that work fine. If you have a Windows computer, one of these programs is already on it.

Also good are all-around programs such as ClarisWorks and Microsoft Works. Word-processing programs with graphics (described above) will work fine in most cases, though they usually lack some of the fancier special effects (such as the spray-paint can or stamps and clip art). Often you need to click a button or choose a command from the menu to turn on your graphics toolbar.

PowerPoint is a popular program you can draw with, though it's really designed to make slide shows. Similarly, PageMaker is designed for laying out documents but has graphics tools that work for drawing. (It's pretty complicated, though.)

There are many expensive and fancy graphics programs that can make beautiful, professional-quality images—such as Illustrator, FreeHand, CorelDraw, Harvard Graphics, and so forth—but they are too hard for most kids (and for many grownups!). You don't really need anything that fancy for the projects in this book. Other graphics programs, like Photoshop, are designed for more specific tasks (touching up photos, in this case) and are too hard to use for these projects.

In general, if a graphics program costs much more than $100 (as of 1998), it's probably too complicated for these projects. PageMaker might be an exception.

Web browser programs (Netscape, Internet Explorer)

If you want to look at the World Wide Web, you will need two things: an account that connects you to the Internet and a special program that lets you look at the Web pages on it. (When people talk about going on the Internet, they usually mean looking at the World Wide Web.)

You may be able to use the computers at school to go on the Web. At home, you need to talk with your parents about getting an account, either with a national company such as America Online, or with a local Internet service provider (or ISP). Local ISPs are usually much cheaper, charging (in 1998) about $20 per month for unlimited time on the Internet. The account also will give your family an E-mail address.

Once that is set up, you will need a Web browser to help you look at the Web pages. The company that gives you your account often will give you a browser for free. The most popular are Microsoft's Internet Explorer and Netscape Navigator. As of 1998 both browsers are free, but this may change, so be sure to check with your Internet service provider for details.

This sounds very complicated, but once you are set up, Web browsers are very easy to use. Most students will have already used these programs at school; the differences between them are minor. Netscape and Internet Explorer have built-in E-mail programs, but many people use a separate program such as Eudora instead. Be sure to check with your parents first about when and how you are allowed to use the family E-mail account.

Page layout programs (desktop publishing)

These range from very simple (PrintShop and Microsoft Publisher) to more complicated (PageMaker). All are designed to let you lay out publication-quality documents, such as newsletters, brochures, even catalogs or magazines. They are also "object-oriented," which means that everything (text, pictures, movies) is an "object" that can be resized and moved quickly using the mouse.

For the projects in this book, word-processing programs with graphics work just as well as page layout programs, and are easier to learn. You won't have as much control over the look of your layout, but you won't need it, either.

Multimedia programs

Multimedia programs are designed to combine words, sounds, pictures, and even video into computer slide shows or animated movies. Some popular examples include KidPix Studio, PowerPoint, HyperStudio, and Hypercard. Some, like Macromind Director, are very fancy and complicated (and expensive!).

You could use these to do simple word processing and drawing. Obviously, you would just make one single slide and print it out. But the real goal of most of these programs is to make slide shows or movies, usually from pictures and sounds you have already made in other programs.

You can make a lot of fun projects with these programs, but they usually involve a lot of steps and are pretty complicated. Plus, different programs do things very differently. Therefore, this book doesn't use them much—they are a topic for another book. But if you have one of these programs, such as PowerPoint, don't be afraid to try it on your own, using the manual or online help if you like. They aren't that difficult, and they're lots of fun.

You probably already have the software needed to do the following projects. If not, start with the ones you can do, then ask your friends for recommendations of current software titles so you can do the rest of the projects.

Section *I*

DRAWING

Computers make it easier to draw well. You can try to draw a line or a picture several times, erasing it every time if you don't like it and saving it to disk when you do. Once you have a good drawing, you can add it to your collection, easily copy it and send it to people, and put it into your letters, cartoons, and anyplace else you can imagine.

YOU ARE AN ARTIST!
Basic Drawing on the Computer

The following project gives you a chance to try out the drawing tools in your software program. They might be new for you, but they're easy and we'll use them throughout this book. Try drawing your house or apartment building to test your skills!

What You Do

1 Open your graphics program or word-processing program with graphics. Create a new file. (Usually programs do this automatically. If not, FILE:NEW.) In all-around programs like Microsoft Works or ClarisWorks, make sure you create a Draw or Drawing document.

2 Find your drawing tools. If you are using a word processor with graphics, you probably need to turn on a graphics toolbar. It will usually be a button on your toolbar.

If not, you will need to use a command such as WINDOW:SHOW TOOLS.

 One of the ways to get drawing tools on your screen is to click on a symbol like this.

3 Draw a rectangle for the house. Click on the rectangle tool, then click on the screen. Keep holding down the mouse button as you drag to the right, then up. If you make a mistake, go to EDIT:UNDO and try again!

 These tools work the same way. One draws rectangles and squares, another draws circles, and another draws rounded rectangles.

 Remember, in order to draw perfect squares or circles, hold down the SHIFT key before you begin to draw.

4 Draw a roof for the house using the irregularly shaped polygon drawing tool.

The irregular polygon tool.

 Remember to double-click to make it stop drawing.

Using the mouse, click on a corner of the house and let go of the mouse button.

Every time you click, the computer will draw a new line to that point. Click again when you have the side as long as you want. Click again when you have the second side as long as you want. Click the mouse again to draw a line closing the triangle. You might have to double-click the mouse to stop drawing lines.

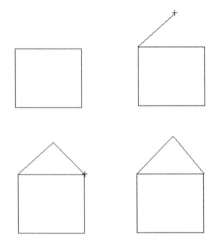

5 To fill the roof with a pattern and color, first select the triangle. To select the triangle, click on the arrow tool in the toolbox, then click on the triangle. Now choose colors and patterns until you have a roof you like! If you are in a paint program, just choose a fill color, then select the paint bucket and click in the middle of the triangle to fill it.

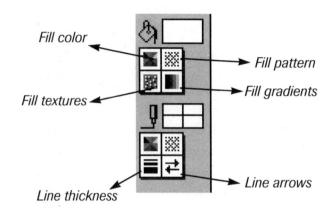

Fill color
Fill pattern
Fill textures
Fill gradients
Line thickness
Line arrows

6 Add some windows. Select the rectangle tool. If you want these to be perfect squares, hold down the SHIFT key while you draw.

7 After you draw a window, click on the fill pattern and choose a pattern. Click on the pen color and choose a pattern that has horizontal lines.

8 Draw a tree. Select a freehand tool, which usually looks like one of these:

A variety of tools with which you can draw freely.

Choose a brown shade for your tree trunk. Click and drag the mouse (holding down the mouse) to draw it.

9 Copy (EDIT:COPY) and paste (EDIT:PASTE) one tree. Click on the tree and drag it to move it. Now you have two trees! Make as many as you want.

10 Draw the circle part of the sun, using the circle drawing tool. Hold down the SHIFT key as you draw it to make sure the sun is round. Then click on the circle and fill it with a yellow shade and a pattern.

11 Make the pen color yellow. To draw rays, choose the straight line draw tool.

Click and drag the mouse to draw lines, making rays around the sun. You might have to reselect the line tool after drawing each line.

For drawing lines. To draw straight lines with other drawing tools, hold the SHIFT key down when drawing.

12 Add anything else you want to your house, such as flowers, a dog, your family, or a mailbox. Experiment with other drawing tools.

PERSONAL ART GALLERY
Clip Art

2

Clip art is what we call pictures that are already drawn and ready for you to put into letters, pictures, newspapers, and other things you make on the computer. Originally clip art was printed on paper, and people would cut out (or "clip") a picture with scissors and paste it onto a sheet of paper. Nowadays, clip art is usually on computers, but we still use the old words—"cut" and "paste"—as if we were using scissors and glue.

In this project, you will make your own art gallery of clip art. You can save copies of the images you draw in your clip art file, trade pictures with your friends, and include clip art from some programs such as Microsoft Word, PowerPoint, and Hyperstudio (on the Macintosh) or from the Internet. Looking at one of these other collections also gives you good ideas for what to put into your clip art file, even if you don't like any of their pictures. You can use clip art in many of the projects in this book.

Creatures

Everyday objects

What You Do

Using a word processor with graphics, or a graphics program

1 If you don't have a clip art folder yet, create one in a convenient place on your hard drive. Give it the name "Clipart." (If you haven't made folders before, ask a parent or teacher for help.) It's very important that you remember where to find your clip art folder.

2 Open your word processor with graphics or graphics program.

3 Create a new file. (Usually programs do this automatically. If not, FILE:NEW.) In all-around programs like Microsoft Works or ClarisWorks, make sure you create a Draw or Drawing document.

4 Draw your picture on the screen.

5 Save the file (FILE:SAVE).

6 You can bring in pictures from other programs, too. Using a select tool, copy (EDIT:COPY) the picture in another program, then quit that program. Open your clip art file and paste (EDIT:PASTE) the picture.

7 Save the file (FILE:SAVE).

8 If you have a lot of pictures, you should keep the same kind of pictures together in separate sub-folders of your clip art folder so it's easier to find them in the future. A sub-folder is just a folder that's inside another folder.

For example, you could group all your pictures alphabetically, putting all those starting with "a" together in one folder, or you could group them by subject (like "animals" or "people"). If you have a lot of clip art, you could make a list in a different file to help you remember which pictures you have, and which folder each one is in.

9 If you want to make another picture, create a new file (FILE:NEW), draw the picture, and save it into your clip art folder.

Inserting Clip Art into Another File

1 Open the file where you want to put the clip art.

2 Switch back to the file where your clip art is.

If you are using a PC, click the symbol in the upper right-hand corner that looks like a minus sign (minimize button). This will reduce your document to an icon at the bottom of the screen. Then open up your clip art file.

If you are using a Mac, click on the symbol in the upper right-hand corner of the screen that looks like a small computer (the multifinder). In the menu that appears, choose Finder. Open your hard drive, then open the file with your clip art.

3 Select the picture you want by clicking on it or using a selection tool.

4 Copy the picture (EDIT:COPY).

5 When finished with your clip art, quit the clip art program.

6 Switch back to your other program.

If you are using a PC, click on the icon at the bottom of the screen. This will return your document to the screen.

If you are using a Mac, click on the multifinder again. In the menu that appears, choose the name of the program you want to return to.

7 Paste the picture where you want it (EDIT:PASTE).

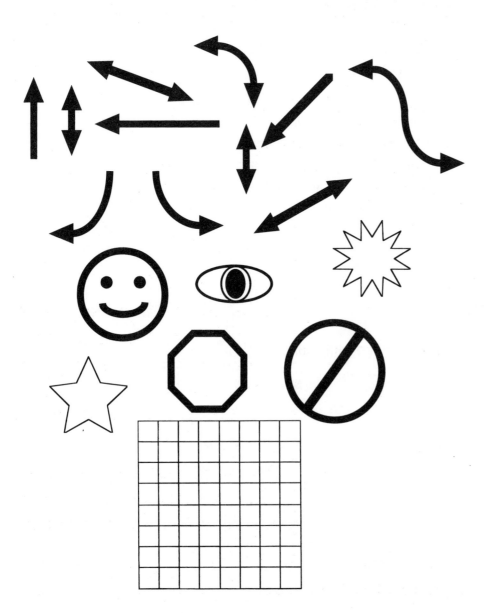

Things to WATCH OUT For!

Pictures that are too big. Keep pictures small. Small pictures can always be enlarged later.

Variations:

● In addition to drawings, you can save useful symbols, such as arrows, stars, eyes, and smiley faces, in your clip art file.

● The grids and boxes you will create in other sections of this book, or anything that takes a long time to make and that you may want to use again, could be saved in your clip art file.

FRAME-UPS
Borders

3

Anything you make on the computer will look better if you surround it with a fancy border or frame. Instead of making special ones each time, you can save a few so they are ready to use for special occasions. Save them in a special folder in your clip art collection.

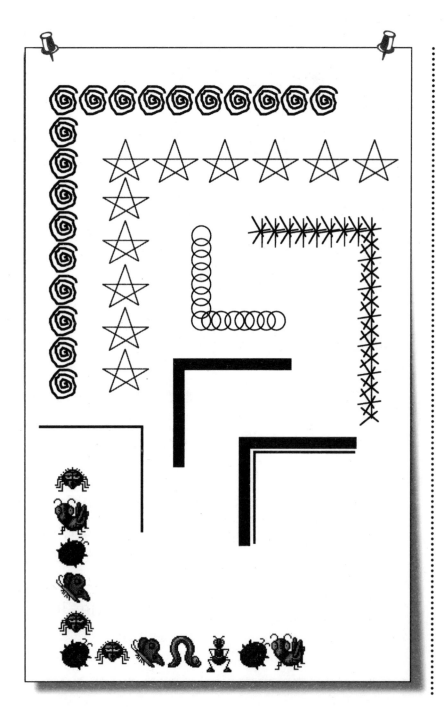

paper (fancy paper if you like)

crayons, colored pencils, or markers

What You Do

Making a New Border or Frame

1 Open your program.

2 Create a new file. (Usually the program does this automatically. If not, FILE:NEW.)

3 Start drawing your border around the outside edge of the page. You can use straight lines and rectangles, or draw a freehand pattern. Or you can copy a small picture from your clip art file and paste it many times all around the edges to make your border.

4 Save your file (FILE:SAVE) with a name like "Border" or "Frames" and put it in your clip art folder, if you have one (see page 8).

Using One of Your Borders or Frames

1 Open the program and file that contain your frames and borders.

2 Find a border that you like. You can either copy it (select it, then EDIT:COPY) and paste it into a new document (FILE:NEW, then EDIT:PASTE), or just make a copy of the entire file (FILE:SAVE AS).

3 Now draw or write what you want in the blank area inside the border. If you have things in another file that you want to put there, copy and paste them in.

4 Save your file with a new name (FILE:SAVE AS) and print it out.

Variations:

- You can use the frames in many of the later projects in this book, including Personalize It: Your Own Stationery (see page 30) and Make a Million: Money and Coupons (see page 33).

- You can also make memo pads (From the Desk of . . .), phone message notes, shopping lists, and other printed forms.

Things to WATCH OUT For!

Pieces of your border getting cut off.

Most printers have a "printable area," which is often everything a half-inch or more inside the edges of your paper. Any part of your border that is outside this area, or is outside the margins, won't be printed. You can fix this problem by making the margins smaller or by moving the border away from the edge of your paper. Change the margins by going to FILE:PAGE SETUP and change all margins to 0.5 inches. That's usually as small as you can go.

ASKY ART
Pictures Made from Letters

Before there were graphics programs for computers, people figured out how to draw a kind of picture using only the letters and other characters on the keyboard. This is called "ASCII art" (pronounced "asky") because the computer codes for letters were invented by a group called ASCII. ASCII is a programming code that stands for **A**merican **s**tandard **c**ode for **i**nformation **i**nterchange.

It's amazing what can be "drawn" using only letters. ASCII art takes only a very small amount of computer memory and travels very quickly. For example, you can put it directly into any E-mail, instead of having to attach a graphics file and open it up separately. (Some E-mail programs let you put pictures directly in an E-mail, but many people won't be able to see these yet.)

Asky art is a nice way to send lighthearted messages (such as a bouquet of roses as a get well message).

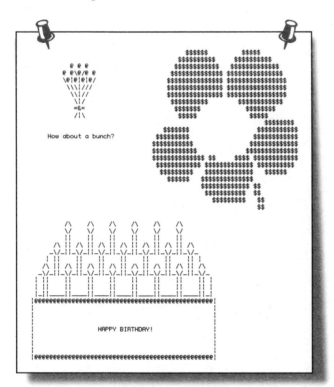

Things You'll Need

paper

pencil

E-mail access (optional)

What You Do

1 Make a quick sketch on paper (grid paper if you have it) of how you plan to make your drawing. Use little x's that are all the same size to draw it. Remember, you will have to draw this from top to bottom, one line across at a time.

2 For example, say you wanted to draw a totem pole. First, you'd probably want to refer to one in a book, like this.

A totem pole is a tall column, so you'll need to write about 35 to 40 lines. Draw about 6 x's across the middle of the page in the same place on every line.

Draw the arms across your existing pole, a little above the middle. To draw the arms of the totem pole, start far to the left and draw one whole row of x's , about 36, across. The bottoms of the arms are narrower than the

```
      xxxxxx
      xxxxxx
      xxxxxx
      xxxxxx
      xxxxxx
      xxxxxx
xxxxxxxxxxxxxxxxxxxxxxxxxxxxxxxxxxxxx
xxxxxxxxxxxxxxxxxxxxxxxxxxxxxxxxxx
xxxxxxxxxxxxxxxxxxxxxxxxxxxxxxx
      xxxxxx
      xxxxxx
      xxxxxx
      xxxxxx
      xxxxxx
      xxxxxx
      xxxxxx
      xxxxxx
      xxxxxx
```

```
    ^       ^
    ^^     ^^
    ^####^
   x^xx^x
   x@xx@x
  <<xxxxxx>>
    xxxxxx
    x-OO-x
MMxxxxxxxxxxxxxxxxxxxxxxxxxxxxxxxxxxxxxMM
  MxxxxxxxxxxxxxxxxxxxxxxxxxxxxxxxxxxxM
   MxxxxxxxxxxxxxxxxxxxxxxxxxxxxxxxxxM
     VVxxxxVV
     VVxxVV
     xxVVxx
     xxxxxx
     xxxxxx
     xxxxxx
     xxxxxx
    /xxxx\
  _//xxxxxx\\_
```

tops, like wings, so for the second line, only type 34 x's (one less on each side). For the next line, only type 32 x's.

To draw faces on the column of the totem pole, you could experiment with using different characters instead of x. For example, an "O" could be a mouth, "@" could be eyes, and ")" or "(" could be dimples on either side of the mouth.

3 Open your program.

4 Create a new file. (Usually the program does this automatically. If not, FILE:NEW.)

5 Change the font to a fixed-width font, such as Courier, Courier New, or Monotype. In these fonts, all letters are the same width, even ";" and "w," so they line up more easily and are much easier to draw with.

6 Type the characters line by line and put in spaces where you want a blank. It's easiest to use all x's at first until you get good at this. Other characters change the shading and texture of your drawing.

7 Save your file occasionally (FILE:SAVE). You might need to make changes several times before it comes out right.

8 When you're done, print a copy for yourself, save your file, and E-mail it to some friends.

Things to WATCH OUT For!

Picking an image that is too hard to draw with letters.

Pick something simple and be sure to plan out how it will work first. Really complicated pictures with lots of little details don't work very well.

Variations:

- Try drawing your own name using the correct letters.

```
MM        MM          A          RRRRR      KK        KK
MMMM      MMMM        AA AA       RR   RR    KK      KK
MM MM   MM MM        AA   AA      RR   RR    KK    KK
MM  MM  MM  MM       AA     AA    RR RR      KK  KK
MM   MM MM   MM     AAAAAAAAAAA   RRR        KKKK
MM    MMM    MM    AA        AA   RR RR      KKKK
MM          MM    AA          AA  RR  RR     KK  KK
MM          MM   AA            AA RR   RR    KK    KK
MM          MM  AA              AA RR    RR  KK      KK
MM          MM AA                AA RR     RR KK        KK
```

- Draw pictures of characters from movies or books.

- When you want to get fancier, try different letters and characters to give your picture shading and details.

- Experiment, especially with the characters that aren't letters or numbers. For example, you could use the parentheses ( ) to add dimples to your totem's mouth, or maybe asterisks * for eyes. This guy has braces and is nervous.

```
 ^^^^^        ^^^^^
< @ >        < @ >
          ==
        / - - \        Oh, no!!
         (O)
```

- If you have an E-mail account, you could copy this picture into your "signature file," which is put at the end of every E-mail you send. (Every E-mail program does this differently, so you'll have to ask a parent or teacher for help, or check the manual.) But be careful!! Usually you can't see your "signature," but it is automatically attached to all your E-mails. Don't forget what you're sending people, and don't put anything obnoxious in it!

```
         ___
      (((###)))
```

DRAWING THROUGH THE MIRROR
Symmetrical Pictures

Symmetry is when two sides of something are exactly the same, except reversed—one side is the mirror image of the other. We can make mirror drawings with only half the work of a regular drawing, by copying one half and flipping it over.

You might think your face is symmetrical, but it really isn't. Each side is a little different. If you hold a mirror up along the edge of your nose and make a mirror image of one side of your face, your face will look very different, if not a little weird. Plus, you'll have a mirror on your nose!

Things You'll Need

paper

crayons, colored pencils, or markers

What You Do

1 Open your program.

2 Create a new file. (Usually the program does this automatically. If not, FILE:NEW.)

3 Draw half of a symmetrical picture (such as one side of a butterfly or a heart).

4 Using the appropriate tool, select the picture. Depending on the program, you usually either just click on the graphic, or click on a selection tool and select the graphic. Copy it (EDIT:COPY).

5 Paste the picture next to its twin (EDIT:PASTE).

6 Flip the picture to reverse it. There are specific tools you can use to flip a picture. They are different in different programs, but are often called something like Flip Horizontally, Flip Vertically, or Transform. Experiment with the drawing tools until you turn the second (copied) picture into its mirror image.

7 Drag and move the pictures side by side to complete the picture. Sometimes you will have to draw small lines to connect the two halves.

8 Color your drawing on the computer if you have a color printer.

Drawing through the Mirror **19**

9 Save your file (FILE:SAVE).

10 Print your drawing.

11 If you printed in black and white, color your drawing by hand using crayons, colored pencils, or markers.

Things to WATCH OUT for!

Making the first half of the picture too big. Keep your pictures small enough so you have room to paste the other half of your symmetrical picture.

Variations:

- Some good things to draw with this technique are rockets, robots, and holiday things such as skeletons and pumpkins.

- Try making a mirror image of your name: write out your name using a drawing tool, then flip it over. Put the two versions of your name together. What does the drawing look like? Color it in a fun way to make it look like a clown, a bug, or an alien.

- You can also use mirror writing to write secret messages to your friends (see the section on Secret Codes). Write a message to a friend, then flip it over using the flip tool. Erase the original message and print out the mirror image. Give this to your friends and tell them to hold it up to the mirror to read it.

COLOR YOUR WORLD
Coloring Books

6

A coloring book is another fun and easy thing you can make using a computer. You can color your own pictures, or you can trade with friends.

Things You'll Need

paper

crayons, colored pencils, or markers

stapler

What You Do

1 Open your program.

2 Create a new file. (Usually programs do this automatically. If not, FILE:NEW.)

3 Using the rectangle tool, draw a frame for the coloring book page. It should be almost as big as the whole page.

4 Inside the rectangle, draw a picture using the pencil, straight line, or polygon tool. The picture is only an outline for someone to color in later. Be sure to leave lots of white space inside the lines to color in.

5 Save your picture (FILE:SAVE).

6 Print your picture and color it by hand.

7 Collect a bunch of coloring book pictures and staple them together down the left side and you have an original coloring book. If you want, you can use a sheet with your name written on it ("Bob's Coloring Book") and a fancy border around it (see page 12) as a cover.

• •

Variations:

- You can make a coloring book picture out of a photo if your computer has a scanner. Just scan the photo and outline it, then delete the photo.

- Give coloring books as party favors.

- Take a coloring book to work on in the car or on an airplane.

- Make a coloring book of favorite cartoon characters or action figures.

• •

Things to WATCH OUT For!

Not leaving enough white space for easy coloring. Be sure to draw lots of different large areas to color.

BETTER THAN BATMAN
Your Own Comic Book

7

Comic books and comic strips are fun to read, and it's even more fun to write your own! Because comics use the same pictures over and over (backgrounds and characters, for example), computers make it a lot easier to draw them.

Things You'll Need

paper

crayons, colored pencils, or markers

stapler, or needle and thread

What You Do

1 Open your program.

2 Create a new file. (Usually programs do this automatically. If not, FILE:NEW.)

3 Using the rectangle tool, draw a frame for the entire page (the outside). It should be almost as large as the whole page.

4 You will be making six smaller squares of equal size on the screen. First draw one square. Then, using the select tool, select the first square you drew (click carefully with the tip of the arrow on the edge of the square). Copy it (EDIT:COPY) and paste it (EDIT:PASTE) to the right of the first square.

5 Continue to cut and paste until you have a total of six squares on the page. This is your template, a blank form that you can use for all your pages.

6 Save the file (FILE:SAVE). You may want to add it to your clip art collection, too.

7 Create a new file. (Usually programs do this automatically. If not, FILE:NEW.)

8 Copy your template and paste it into the new file once for every page you want to draw.

9 For each scene in your comic, start by drawing a background, just like in a newspaper comic strip. (For example, it might be a house and the sun, or a mountain.) When you're done, copy the background into your clip art gallery, too.

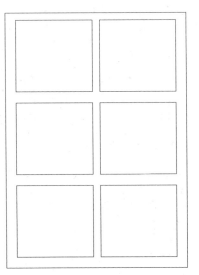

10 Paste your background into every panel that will have that background. After you paste it in, you can go back in and change each one slightly if you need to. For example, you could change the time on a clock or make the sun go down to show that time has passed.

11 Use the drawing tools on your computer to draw your main characters and copy them into your clip art gallery.

12 Paste your characters in wherever they should appear. Again, you can go back and change them a little (make them smile or frown, for example, and add words). You can even draw them completely differently if you want (for example, if there's a big fight, you may need to draw them moving all around). But whenever they look about the same, paste them in from clip art.

13 Make a cover page by drawing a rectangle at the top for the name of the comic strip and your name. Leave a bigger rectangle below that for one big picture that you draw in.

14 Color the pictures in your comic on the computer if you have a color printer.

15 Once you're done, save your file to your hard drive (FILE:SAVE) and make a backup copy on a disk.

16 Print the pages out, put them all together in order with the cover on top, and staple or sew them together.

17 If you printed in black and white, color in your comic with crayons, colored pencils, or markers.

Variations:

- Print on colored paper or cut and paste the frames onto colored construction paper.

- If you're going on vacation and you can't take your computer, print out a bunch of sheets with just the frame of your cartoon—the boxes and borders that you draw your cartoon in. Then you can draw the actual cartoons by hand.

- Instead of making up characters, you could draw a comic about your friends or family members. Or draw a comic about a favorite character from a book or movie!

- In your comic strip, you can do anything you want, like make your dog talk and drive a car, or go back in time, or fly through outer space. Have fun with it!!

PLACE KEEPERS
Bookmarks

If you like to read or know someone who does, make some bookmarks to hold your place in the book you are reading. Decorate these in silly ways or personalize them with names and pictures.

Fold here

What You Do

1 Open your program.

2 Create a new file. (Usually the program does this automatically. If not, FILE:NEW.)

3 Draw a rectangle about 5 inches (20 cm) wide and 4 inches (15 cm) tall. (Many drawing programs and some word processors have rulers you can measure this against, but the exact size doesn't really matter.)

4 Draw a line sideways through the middle of the rectangle, dividing it in half. (This is where you will fold the bookmark.)

5 Draw or write things on both sides of the rectangle. For example, on one side write your name and on the other draw characters from your favorite book.

6 If you have a color printer, use color on the computer for your drawings and to fill in the letters.

7 Save your file (FILE:SAVE) and print.

Things You'll Need
paper
crayons, colored pencils, or markers
clear contact paper (optional)

8 If you printed in black and white, color in your drawing with crayons, colored pencils, or markers.

9 Cut on the lines of the rectangle.

10 Fold along the line in the middle of the rectangle.

11 Glue, staple, or paper-clip the book-mark shut. If you can, laminate it with contact paper to waterproof it.

Things to WATCH OUT For!

Drawing outside the rectangle. That part will get cut off when you cut out your bookmark.

Variation:

- Make holiday gifts for all the readers you know. Personalize each one with names and pictures of things the person likes.

Personalize It
Your Own Stationery

9

You can make your own stationery with your name, address, and phone number, and even include your E-mail address. You print out just the letterhead, and then later you can use it for handwritten letters or for writing on your word processor. To use your stationery for word-processed letters, just put the letterhead in your printer where you usually put blank paper. Make sure you leave enough blank space at the top of the document so you don't print on top of the printing already on your stationery. You may also

Anna Casserly
1123 Stuart Lane
San Jose, CA 94135
415-555-1212
annac@fun.edu

have to try a few times before you figure out which way to put the paper in the printer so that the letter is right side up and on the right side of the page.

Things You'll Need

paper
access to a Xerox machine (optional)

What You Do

1 Open your program.

2 Create a new file. (Usually programs do this automatically. If not FILE:NEW.)

3 Turn on text centering. Usually there is a command called Justification or Alignment, which you set to center. Or click the centering button.

4 Type your full name on one line, hit RETURN (or ENTER) and type your street address, then press RETURN (or ENTER) and type your city, state, and ZIP. Type your phone number and E-mail address on separate lines below the address, if you want.

5 Format your text, changing the size, style, font, and color (if possible).

6 Add art next to the address, if you want. You can either draw something directly on your stationery, or add something from your clip art collection (see page 7).

7 Draw a line below everything you've typed and drawn, and press the RETURN (or ENTER) key twice.

8 Save your stationery as a template, if your program allows that, or as a regular document. Don't type a full letter in your stationery file; you want to save just the name and address so you can use it again and again. If you want to type a letter directly in this file, save a copy of the file under a different name first (FILE:SAVE AS).

9 Print out a bunch of copies of your stationery, or print one copy and make more on a copy machine. You can write a letter by hand on your paper or use this paper in your printer to print a word-processed letter on it.

Variations:

- You can make memo pads (From the Desk of . . .), phone message notes, shopping lists, To Do lists, and other printed forms. You can make scratch paper or notepads by selecting all of the items on the letterhead (EDIT:SELECT ALL), shrinking the items (if your software allows), and making four copies on one page. Print the page and cut out the four copies.

- Make a letterhead for the job you want to do when you grow up: "Carol Sauer, Astronaut, 12 Rocket Lane, Cape Canaveral, FL 12345"

- Draw a self-portrait and put it in your letterhead. If you have access to a scanner or digital camera, add a current photo of yourself.

Things to WATCH OUT For!

1 Never give your address or phone number to strangers, or send them letterhead that includes your address or phone number. If you're not sure whether it's okay, always ask your parents first.

2 The text may be covered by the pictures. Try clicking on the picture (so you see little black squares around the sides of the picture). In the software, there is usually a command like "SEND TO BACK" on a menu named "Arrange," "Object," or "Element," or a button for "Send to Back" on a drawing toolbar. This will put the picture on a layer underneath the words.

MAKE A MILLION
Money and Coupons

10

Make your own fake money to bet in card games, or make coupons to give to friends and family members as presents. (Your coupon could say, "Good for doing the dishes one time," or "Good for one foot rub.")

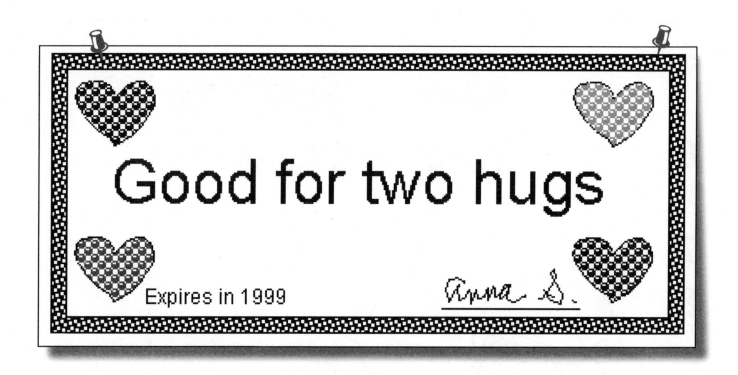

Good for two hugs

Expires in 1999

Anna S.

Things You'll Need

paper

crayons, colored pencils, or markers

What You Do

1 Open your program.

2 Create a new file. (Usually the program does this automatically. If not, FILE:NEW.)

3 Draw a large rectangle in the middle of the screen.

4 Put a fancy border just inside your rectangle (see page 11).

5 Draw a circle or oval in the middle of the large rectangle. This will be where you type what the coupon or your money is worth.

6 Decorate your coupon with pictures, drawings, or clip art (see page 7). You might look at some real money to get ideas.

7 Save your file (FILE:SAVE).

8 Print as many copies of the coupon as you want to give.

• •

Variations:

● These coupons make great birthday gifts:

"One visit to the movies"

"One computer lesson (for Mom or Dad)"

"One car washing"

"Cook one dinner"

"One hug"

"One cleaning up after dinner"

• •

Things to WATCH OUT For!

1 Counterfeit coupons! To make sure nobody is printing up their own copies, put your signature on each coupon after you print it out.

2 Don't ever try to use fake money at a real store. Counterfeiting is a VERY serious crime, even for kids.

MAKE IT MOVE
Flip Books

11

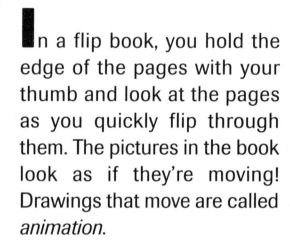

In a flip book, you hold the edge of the pages with your thumb and look at the pages as you quickly flip through them. The pictures in the book look as if they're moving! Drawings that move are called *animation*.

It's fun to make your own flip books. You may be amazed when you realize how many little stages it takes just to show someone walking.

What You Do

1 Open your program.

2 Create a new file. (Usually programs do this automatically. If not, FILE:NEW.)

3 Make a box around 2–3 inches (10–15 cm) square to serve as a frame.

4 Make a simple drawing of a stick figure inside the frame.

5 Copy the image (both stick figure and frame) and paste it on another part of the page. There should be room to put several on a page. Leave some extra space at the top of each frame for the staples or thread. If they are in even rows and columns, it will be easier to cut them up.

6 Edit the picture slightly in each frame to make the arms and legs move, so that it looks as if the figure is running (the left leg and right arm move forward while right leg and left arm move backward, for example).

Things You'll Need

paper
scissors
stapler, or needle and thread

7 For each frame, move the entire figure slightly to the right so that your runner will move across the page. You can even make it look as if he runs off the page!

8 If you want the runner to run a long way, copy the whole sequence and paste it again at the end. Repeat as many times as you want.

9 Print out your pages.

10 Cut up the framed pictures so they're all the same size, with extra space at the top.

11 Put your pictures in order and flip through them to make sure they look the way you want.

12 When you're ready, staple or sew the pages together through the extra space at the top.

13 Show your flip book to someone else and ask them what they see.

Things to WATCH OUT For!

1 Getting the pages mixed up. It may help you to number each frame in the extra space at the top before you cut it out.

2 Changing the picture too much between frames. If the changes are too big, they will happen too fast for you to see. Your flip book will look better if you make more pages with smaller changes.

Variations:

- A flip book can show anything, of course: a rocket flying, a wedding, a horse race. Try as many new things as you can.

- Add color to the frames, either on the computer or by hand after you print the pages out.

Section II

WRITING

The greatest thing about writing on a computer is that you can easily make changes later without retyping everything (if you remember to SAVE). You can print out copies of written work, get comments on it from family or friends, and then make changes (if you want) to your computer file.

Once you've finished the writing part, take some time to make your work look as good as it reads. Change the font, size, and style. Add color to the words (use a color printer if you have one, or use crayons, markers, or colored pencils).

Here's a collection of fun ideas to get you writing.

EXTRA! EXTRA!
Your Own Newspaper

12

Everybody likes to read the newspaper. But it's even better when the news is written by you! Create a format for your newspaper on the computer, then take it with you to report on school or on your vacation. You can have sections for headline news, weather, advertisements, special events, cartoons, sports, even recipes. Conduct interviews with family, friends, or people you meet and put them in your paper. If you want, you can have an editorial column and let different people submit columns to your paper.

Eileen's Newspaper

June 8, 1998

HEADLINE NEWS

SPORTS

WEATHER

QUOTE OF THE DAY

Things You'll Need

paper

stapler

pen

crayons, colored pencils, or markers

What You Do

1 Open your program.

2 Create a new file. (Usually programs do this automatically. If not, FILE:NEW.)

3 Draw a frame for the outside of the newspaper, using the rectangle tool. It should be almost as big as the whole page.

4 You can make your page print the normal way, taller than it is wide. This is called "portrait orientation" because it looks like a portrait painting. Or you can change it to "landscape orientation," which got its name because it is wider than it is tall, like a landscape painting. On most programs, the command to change this is FILE: PAGE SETUP.

5 At the top of the page, draw a large rectangle for the title and date of your newspaper. Use a fancy border (see page 11) for this section.

6 Type your title in a large, interesting font.

7 Draw other rectangles for ads, a cartoon, and articles. Make columns, different-shaped boxes, and other interesting sections. (To get ideas, look at a real newspaper or magazine.)

8 Save the file (FILE:SAVE) and print.

9 Make more pages the same way, with columns of different shapes and sizes.

10 Print several copies of each page, so you'll have enough to do a bunch of daily or weekly papers.

11 Staple the pages of your newspaper together on one side.

12 Carry your newspaper and a pen with you and write down whatever interesting news you notice. Draw some pictures in it, too.

13 When you've finished writing the news, decorate your pages with crayons, colored pencils, or markers.

Things to WATCH OUT For!

Making boxes that are too small.

Be sure you leave enough room to write as much as you want. If you don't fill up all the space with your writing, you can always add a drawing.

Variations:

- Print on legal-sized or other different-sized paper.
- Print on colored or other fancy paper.
- If you have a copier, copy pages double-sided.
- Include clip art or scan in photos to illustrate stories.
- You could write your entire newspaper on the computer, if you have a page layout program like PageMaker or Microsoft Publisher. This is much more difficult, though. Or you can type a less fancy newspaper on your word processor. You won't be able to fill in different boxed areas if you try it this way, so the paper won't look as interesting.

ROUND ROBIN
Circular E-mail Chat

13

This is a great way to chat with friends who have E-mail. You can pick any subject you want your friends' opinions on and have them pass it on. The E-mail goes around in a circle until it gets back to you, with everybody's comments.

This is an especially good way to chat with friends or family in other cities. It is much cheaper than phone calls and faster than letters.

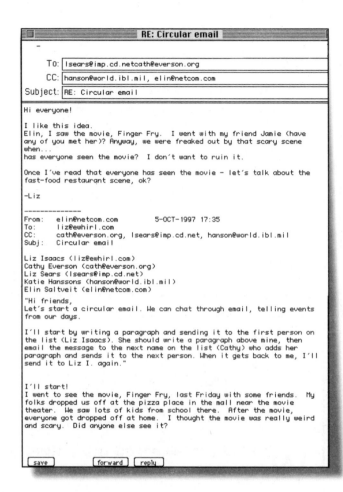

```
┌──────────────── RE: Circular email ─────────────────┐
│ □ ─                                                   │
│                                                       │
│   To: │lsears@imp.cd.netcath@everson.org          │  │
│   CC: │hanson@world.ibl.mil, elin@netcom.com      │  │
│ Subject: │RE: Circular email                      │  │
│                                                       │
│ Hi everyone!                                          │
│                                                       │
│ I like this idea.                                     │
│ Elin, I saw the movie, Finger Fry.  I went with my    │
│ friend Jamie (have any of you met her)? Anyway, we    │
│ were freaked out by that scary scene when...          │
│ has everyone seen the movie?  I don't want to ruin it.│
│                                                       │
│ Once I've read that everyone has seen the movie -     │
│ let's talk about the fast-food restaurant scene, ok?  │
│                                                       │
│ -Liz                                                  │
│                                                       │
│ --------------                                        │
│ From:  elin@netcom.com      5-OCT-1997 17:35          │
│ To:    liz@ewhirl.com                                 │
│ CC:    cath@everson.org, lsears@imp.cd.net,           │
│        hanson@world.ibl.mil                           │
│ Subj:  Circular email                                 │
│                                                       │
│ Liz Isaacs (liz@ewhirl.com)                           │
│ Cathy Everson (cath@everson.org)                      │
│ Liz Sears (lsears@imp.cd.net)                         │
│ Katie Hanssons (hanson@world.ibl.mil)                 │
│ Elin Saltveit (elin@netcom.com)                       │
│                                                       │
│ "Hi friends,                                          │
│ Let's start a circular email. We can chat through     │
│ email, telling events from our days.                  │
│                                                       │
│ I'll start by writing a paragraph and sending it to   │
│ the first person on the list (Liz Isaacs). She should │
│ write a paragraph above mine, then email the message  │
│ to the next name on the list (Cathy) who adds her     │
│ paragraph and sends it to the next person. When it    │
│ gets back to me, I'll send it to Liz I. again."       │
│                                                       │
│ I'll start!                                           │
│ I went to see the movie, Finger Fry, last Friday with │
│ some friends.  My folks dropped us off at the pizza   │
│ place in the mall near the movie theater.  We saw     │
│ lots of kids from school there.  After the movie,     │
│ everyone got dropped off at home.  I thought the      │
│ movie was really weird and scary.  Did anyone else    │
│ see it?                                               │
│                                                       │
│ [save]          [forward] [reply]                     │
└───────────────────────────────────────────────────────┘
```

• •

Things You'll Need

E-mail account (and a bunch of friends with E-mail)

• •

What You Do

1 Open your E-mail account.

2 Create a new E-mail message.

3 Decide who will be part of the circular E-mail letter. Type a list of names and E-mail addresses at the top of the message. Make sure your name is at the bottom.

Liz Isaacs (liz@ewhirl.com)

Cathy Everson (cath@everson.org)

Liz Sears (lsears@imp.cd.net)

Katie Hanssons (hanson@world.ibl.mil)

Elin Saltveit (elin@realchange.org)

4 You'll want to give directions for how to keep the letter moving along. You could type something like the following:

Hi friends,

Let's start a circular E-mail. We can chat through E-mail, telling the things that happen to us.

I'll start by writing a paragraph and sending it to the first person on the list

(Liz Isaacs). She should write a paragraph above mine, then E-mail the message to the next name on the list (Cathy), who adds her paragraph and sends it to the next person. When it gets back to me, I'll send it to Liz I. again.

5 Start the circular E-mail with a paragraph about something that's happened to you recently—or an update on what's been going on. Maybe you want to ask a question like, "What do you think of the new math teacher?" Maybe you just want to tell your friends something neat that happened that day.

6 Send this E-mail to the first person on your list.

7 If the E-mail is getting too big when you get it back, you can delete everything before your last comment, but leave everybody's last paragraph so you can remember what everybody is talking about. Or save that E-mail and start a new one.

Variations:

- Use a circular E-mail letter for birthday wishes. Start it off with your birthday congratulations for the person, and have all your friends add to it. The last person on the list should send it to the person having the birthday.

- Send an E-mail joke list. Start with one joke, and have everyone add one joke as they pass it along.

Things to WATCH OUT For !

Writing anything you don't want a lot of other people to see. Don't say anything that's secret, or too mean. Even if you make everyone promise not to show these E-mails to anyone who isn't on the list, they may slip up and send it to someone else by mistake!

ONCE UPON A TIME
Story Chains

14

In a story chain, one person starts a story, someone else writes the next part, and so on. When it's your turn, you should only look at the part that the last person wrote.

The story can take really unexpected turns! It's a great way to produce neat, scary, or mysterious stories.

I crept down the stairs after I heard a shrill sound coming from the basement. I was in my flannel pajamas, carrying the biggest flashlight I could find. I don't know why I went alone, but it was in the middle of the night and I wasn't thinking clearly.

Halfway down the stairs, I stopped and saw a shadow down below. I could hear my heart thumping in my ears. I thought my loud gulps could be heard throughout the house. I noticed a new mark on the banister near me. A splotch of blue paint? I continued down the staircase.

On the last step of the staircase, my weight on the step made a loud creaking sound. It made me gasp and jump to the ground below. Just as I was about to turn the corner and walk toward the basement door the doorbell rang.

Things You'll Need

paper
You might need several disks to make copies for everybody, or it might be easier to E-mail them a copy.

What You Do

1 Open your word-processing program.

2 Create a new file. (Usually the program does this automatically. If not, FILE:NEW.)

3 Decide who will go first. That person should start the story with a short paragraph. It should introduce a person or animal, say where he or she is, and describe the situation or something that happens.

4 When the first person is done, the next person should sit at the computer and continue the story. Each person should only read the last person's section.

5 Save the file each time someone finishes (FILE:SAVE).

6 When everyone has had a turn, the last person gets to write the end of the story. When done, he or she should press the RETURN (or ENTER) key twice and type "The End."

7 Read through the story with your family or friends. You can either have one person read the whole story, or everyone can read their own part.

8 Pick a story title and type it at the top of the first page.

9 Press the RETURN (or ENTER) key and type the names of the writers: "By Jake and John and Caroline and Anna."

10 Highlight the title and names and center the text. The command is different in different programs, but it usually says Alignment or Justification, and you set it to center. If there's a button, it usually shows several lines that are centered.

11 Save the changes (FILE:SAVE).

12 Print out enough copies for everybody.

Things to WATCH OUT for!

Changing someone else's section. Even if you think you have a better way, this is a group project, so stick to your own section.

Variations:

● You can make the story longer by having more than one turn each. Just make sure that everybody gets the same number of turns.

● Illustrate the story with new art or art from your clip art file (see page 7).

● If you and your friends can't be together in the same place, you can still do this as a circular E-mail letter (see page 44). Just make sure that the last person E-mails the finished story to everybody.

ACT THE PART
Plays

15

In this project, you and a friend create a play while sitting at the computer. Plays need to have a *setting* (the situation), *characters,* and *dialogue* (a conversation between two or more characters in the play).

You should each make up a character and agree on the setting. Then take turns typing the dialogue. You can add in gestures and actions, too (so-and-so cries, grabs the sword, shrugs, etc.).

Skull Island
A Play by Miriam and Seth

Setting: A small deserted island.

Pirate Miriam has just arrived in a boat and sees a treasure chest. She starts to pick it up.

Pirate Blackbeard:

> Arggh, matey!! That's MY treasure! Hand it over or you will die!

Pirate Miriam:

> In a pig's eye, you lily-livered loser!

They fight. Pirate Miriam picks up the treasure and runs away. Pirate Blackbeard chases after her, yelling.

Things You'll Need   paper

What You Do

1 Open your word-processing program.

2 Create a new file. (Usually the program does this automatically. If not, FILE:NEW.)

3 Talk to your friend about the subject of your play. Think about where it is, what year it is, who the characters are, and what is happening to them. Then decide on a title.

4 At the top of the screen, write the title of your play, and the authors. Then press the RETURN (or ENTER) key twice.

5 Type a short paragraph setting the scene of your play.

6 Save your file (FILE:SAVE).

7 Start writing the dialogue between your characters. Type your character's name, followed by a colon, like this:
> Dave: "Hi, Kirstin. What's new?"

8 Type what Dave says, and include any physical motions you want to include in parentheses or on another line (such as, He sits down at the table). As you write, pretend you are that character and say and do things that he or she would say and do.

9 Press the RETURN (or ENTER) key twice and give the keyboard to the other person. He or she should type his or her character's name, followed by a colon and what that character says and does in response to your character.

10 Continue switching sides, writing a conversation between your characters, until your play is written.

11 When you are done, press the RETURN (or ENTER) key twice and write "The End."

12 Try acting out your play (a rehearsal). Use props, and try to make your voice sound like your character's would.

13 As you act it out, you will probably want to change some things. Make notes on your printout. When you're done rehearsing, you can make the changes on your computer.

Variations:

- Conduct interviews and record your questions and their answers as dialogue. Either type while on the phone with the person you are interviewing, or type from notes or in person. You could type the questions, then let the person being interviewed type or E-mail the answers. Give a copy of what you type to the person you interviewed. Let him or her double-check that you remembered exactly what was said, and make corrections. (It's hard to type or write as fast as people talk, so it's pretty easy to make mistakes.)

- If your family has a video camera you can use or if you can borrow one, make your play into a movie!

14 Save the file again (FILE:SAVE) and print out your final copies.

15 Agree on what props to use and how to act out your play, then perform for friends or family.

Things to WATCH OUT For!

1 Unconvincing characters. Try to think and write like your character. If your character is a grown-up, he or she should talk like a grown-up. Try writing down some actual conversations you hear. This can help you make your dialogue more realistic.

2 Action that is too hard to show. Don't write a scene with a big snowstorm if you don't have a way to make it look like it's snowing. (And ask your parents before doing any special effects that might be really messy or break things!)

AD-LIBS
Fill in the Blanks

16

In this game you write a story and decide to leave out certain key words. Then ask a friend to supply a random list of words that can complete the story—before he or she even reads it. Just tell your friend what kind of word you need. For example, "Give me a list of ten nouns and ten verbs. I'll tell you why later." Then complete your stories with the funniest words on the list. Be sure to print a copy for your friend!

I couldn't find my teeth so I had to shower in the car.

. . . .

Things You'll Need   paper

. . . .

What You Do

1 Open your word-processing program.

2 Create a new file. (Usually the program does this automatically. If not, FILE:NEW.)

3 Write a very short story with some action in it. For example, "I couldn't find my keys so I had to climb in the window."

4 Now go back and erase the key words, usually the subject or object of the sentence (who did what) and the verb (the action). Put an underline there instead.

> "I couldn't find my _____ so I had to _____ in the _____."

5 Figure out what kinds of words can fill in the blanks, and write this under the blank. For this example, you need two nouns (things) and one verb (action).

> "I couldn't find my _____ so I had to
> (noun)
>
> _____ in the _____."
> (verb)   (noun)

6 Ask your friend to make a list of five or ten words for each blank you have. Be sure to tell them what kind of word you need. Don't let your friend see the sentence first!

7 Take your friend's list and your story, and sit down together and fill in the blanks. See how many different stories you can make. Some will be pretty funny!

Variation:

● You could do this by E-mail instead of in person. You could either send your friend the story after he or she E-mails you the list of words, so you could each fill in the blanks separately, or you could fill in the blanks and send your friend the finished stories.

Things to WATCH OUT for!

Make sure your story won't accidentally become dirty or offensive when the blanks are filled in.

Do You See What I See?

A Story about a Picture

17

When you draw a picture, you usually have a story in mind as you draw. But when someone else sees the same picture, he or she might think of a completely different story. It's always amazing to see how different the two stories are!

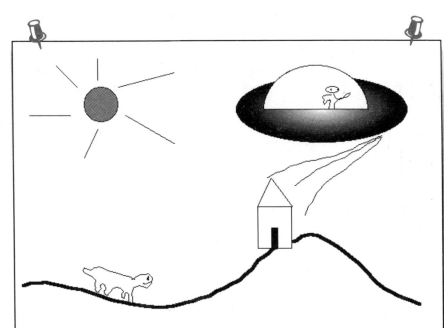

Aliens had just appeared in the sky. I was inside the house but could see my dog, R.D., racing across the field chasing the spaceship. The sun was bright, making the metal of the spaceship shine. Suddenly beams were coming down from the spaceship that lit up the house. I could see the alien working the controls. R.D. was barking and running toward me. I wasn't scared, but wondered what would happen next.

Things You'll Need

paper

What You Do

1 Open your program.

2 Create a new file. (Usually the program does this automatically. If not, FILE:NEW.)

3 Draw a picture. It could just be wild designs, or you could have a story in mind.

4 Show someone the picture on the screen or give him or her a printed copy.

5 Have him or her write a story on the computer describing what he or she thinks is going on in your picture. If you are using a word processor with graphics to draw your picture, he or she can type the story in right under the picture.

6 Save your file (FILE:SAVE).

7 If you drew your picture with a graphics program that doesn't include a word processor, he or she will have to write the story using a word processing program, then print it out. Print out your picture and staple or tape it to the story.

Telling your friend what you think the picture is about. Don't do it! Let him or her come up with his or her own ideas.

Variations:

● Ask your friend to draw a picture at the same time that you do, then swap pictures and each write stories.

● Try having two or more people draw stories about your picture. See how different they are!

● Instead of drawing a real picture, make a random drawing—just a bunch of squiggles and shapes. Ask your friends what they think it looks like.

● If you don't have a drawing program, or want to do this project by yourself, cut out a picture from a magazine or newspaper—without any words under it—and type a story about it on your computer. Print out your story and paste the picture on it.

COOKING UP A STORM!
Make a Cookbook

18

You probably have a few cookbooks full of tasty recipes in your house. How about putting together a cookbook of your family's favorite recipes? Ask all of your friends and relatives. Lots of people have their own special meals that they are great at cooking.

The Gustafson Family
Cookbook

Collected by Cathy Curtis
January 2000

Things You'll Need

paper

stapler

What You Do

1 Open your program.

2 Create a new file. (Usually the program does this automatically. If not, FILE:NEW.)

3 Start typing your first recipe. Type the person's name and the recipe's name at the top, like "Aunt Joan's Chocolate Pie." Type out the recipe as close to the way they gave it to you as possible.

4 If you have any clip art for that kind of food, or a picture of the person who made the recipe, add it to the page.

5 Make a new page for each recipe. The command to create a new page is different in every word processor, but it is usually something like INSERT:NEW PAGE, INSERT:PAGE BREAK, or CTRL + ENTER.

6 When you've got all the recipes, check with each person to make sure you got his or her recipe right. You could mail them printouts of just their recipes, copy them and paste them into an E-mail, or just call them up and read the recipes to them. Correct any mistakes on your computer. When you are done, save the file (FILE:SAVE).

7 Create a table of contents. Include everybody's name and the name of their recipes, followed by the page number it's on. You can just type this out, or use special table-of-contents tools in some advanced word processors (such as Microsoft Word and WordPerfect.) These tools are kind of tricky, though— it's probably easier just to type it up. Save your file when you're done (FILE:SAVE).

8 Make a title page (this will be the cover of the cookbook). Start a new page at the beginning of your file.

9 Center the text. Usually there is a command called Justification or Alignment that you set to center, or click the centering button.

10 Write a title and your name using a large, interesting font.

11 Add some art to your title page. If the program allows, you can draw right on the page, or you can use clip art (see page 7) and add a border (see page 11). There are lots of clip art pictures of different kinds of foods.

12 Save your file (FILE:SAVE).

 Uncle Ted's Easy Meatloaf

You can mix this together in 5 minutes, toss it in a pan, then cook it. It's a meal in itself, but you should probably cook something green to go with it.

Serves 4 hungry people.

Ingredients

1 lb. ground meat (turkey or beef)
1 large onion, chopped into little pieces
2 pieces bread, toasted, and crumbled
2 garlic cloves, chopped or mashed
1/2 teaspoon salt (or more if you like things salty)
1 teaspoon pepper
1 egg
1 cup ketchup

Directions

1. Using your hands, mash together the meat, onion, bread, garlic, salt, and pepper in a bowl.
2. Crack the egg on top and squeeze it into the mixture.
3. Pour 1/2 cup of ketchup into the mixture and combine it with the other stuff.
4. Press the meatloaf goo into a loaf pan.
5. Heat up the oven to 400°.
6. Pour another 1/2 cup of ketchup on top of the meatloaf.
7. Cook for 45 minutes.

13 Print your title page on fancy colored paper, if you have some.

14 Print out the table of contents and recipes on regular paper. Print enough copies of the cookbook for everyone who wants one. Make sure that everybody who gave you a recipe gets a copy.

15 Put the cover on top and a blank piece of fancy paper on the bottom and staple the pages together to make your book.

• •

Variations:

- You could print just one copy of the cookbook, take it to a photocopy shop, and have them make copies. It's more expensive, but they can put on a special cover or a binding for you.

- You could make a cookbook for any group of people, such as your school or church group.

• •

Things to WATCH OUT For!

Nagging people for recipes. It's polite to give everyone a chance to contribute a recipe if they want to, but once you've given them that chance, don't worry if they don't. Just try someone else. It helps to make a deadline for people to send you their recipes. Just be sure to give them enough time.

Section III

GAMES

You can make up new games and collect your old favorites into a book. Use your computer to make some game books before you go on a big trip or just for having fun anytime. You could make a family game book (with games to be created by relatives and immediate family), or make one with your friends.

PICTURE SKELETONS
Connect the Dots

19

Connect-the-dot drawings are fun and easy to make on the computer. To make one, you start with a picture, then put the dots around the edge and erase the original picture. *Voilà!*

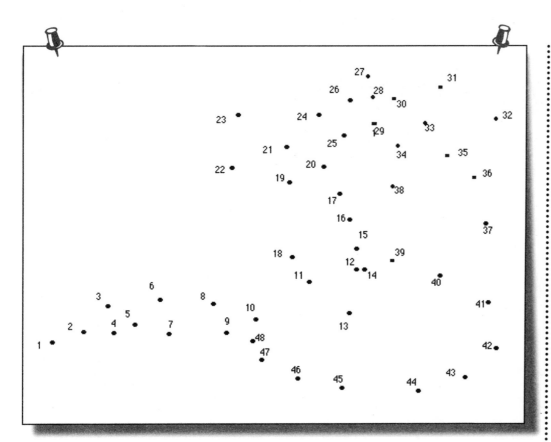

What You Do

1 Open your program.

2 Create a new file. (Usually programs do this automatically. If not, FILE:NEW.)

3 Using a thick line (the paintbrush or pencil tool), draw a picture with a simple outline and no lines in the middle.

4 Once you've finished, put dots around the outside of the line and very close to it, about every ½ inch (1.25 cm).

5 Draw or type numbers next to each dot in the order you want someone to draw.

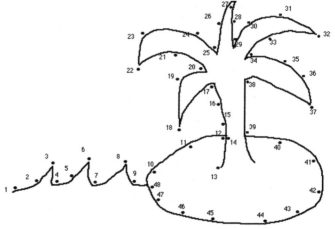

Things You'll Need

paper

crayons, colored pencils, or markers

6 Now "erase" the line of the original drawing. In most programs, you can just click on the line, then press the DELETE (or DEL) key. In paint programs, try clicking on the fill icon (which usually looks like a paint can spilling over or a pen), then click on white for the color. Click right on the line (the active point is the tip of the paint spilling). If too much disappears, click the UNDO button and try again. This should turn the line to white, making it invisible. You might have to click on several segments of the line, because the dots may interrupt filling the entire line, but be sure not to erase any of the dots.

7 Save your file (FILE:SAVE) and print.

8 Test it yourself by using a crayon, colored pencil, or marker to connect the dots. If there are any mistakes, fix them and save your file again.

9 Print your finished picture skeleton, and give it to someone else to fill in.

Things to WATCH OUT For!

Pictures that have too many lines close together. The dots will be hard to place and the numbers will be even harder.

Variation:

● Instead of drawing your own drawing, make a picture skeleton from a piece of clip art. Take a piece of clip art from your collection (see page 7) and copy it onto a new page. Put the dots near the outside edge of the clip art, all around, and then delete the clip art.

MONSTER MASH
Make a Monster

20

This is a project you do with a friend. Each of you imagines a horrible monster and writes up a description of it. Then you draw pictures of each other's monsters. Other people will probably draw a monster that is very different from the one you imagined.

My monster has a body like a dinosaur. He has a small, red, round head and his nose is very short. His ears have points and his teeth and mouth are very big. He has spikes all over his body and round spots all over. He is wearing a tall black hat, spotted gloves on the front feet, and red checked shorts.

What You Do

1 Open your word-processing program.

2 Create a new file. (Usually the program does this automatically. If not, FILE:NEW).

3 Write one paragraph describing a monster. You can make up a name for it if you like. Describe it as carefully as you can so your friend knows what to draw.

4 Save your file and print it out.

5 Trade paragraphs with a friend. You can give him or her a printout, or E-mail it.

Things You'll Need

paper

crayons, colored pencils, or markers

6 Open your graphics program.

7 Create a new file. (Usually the program does this automatically. If not, FILE:NEW.)

8 Draw a picture following your friend's directions. Write a name for the monster on the top.

9 Save your file and print copies for yourself and your friend.

10 Trade your picture for the one your friend drew of your monster.

- You can describe other things besides monsters. Or write a whole story and ask your friend to illustrate it.

- Write a paragraph describing the top of a monster, another paragraph describing the middle, and another describing the bottom. Have two or three other people write these, too. Trade paragraphs so you each have a top section, a middle section, and a bottom section from three different people. Draw the sections and see how the monster tuns out! Compare your pictures and mix up the descriptions again if you want to make new monsters.

A SQUARE DEAL

How Many Squares Can You Find?

21

In this game you will draw a fairly complicated geometric shape and ask people to count how many squares (or other shapes) they can find in it. Try it yourself with the example on the next page.

Remember that one line can be part of both a big square and some smaller squares.

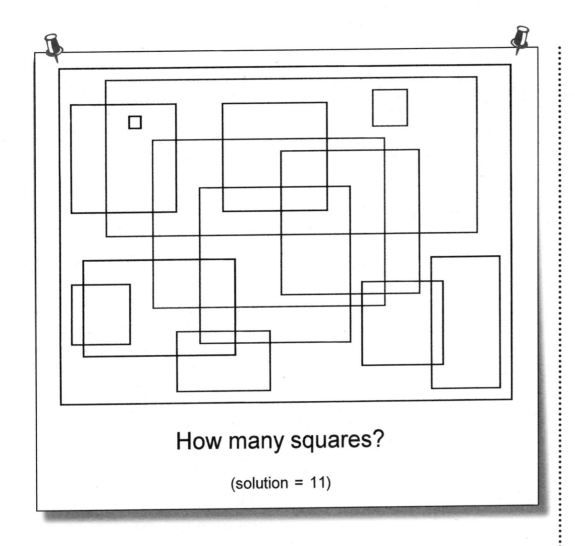

How many squares?

(solution = 11)

Things You'll Need

paper

What You Do

1 Open your program.

2 Create a new file. (Usually the program does this automatically. If not, FILE:NEW.)

3 Draw a picture using many squares and rectangles. To draw squares, hold down the SHIFT key as you begin drawing with the rectangle tool. Be sure you let go of the mouse before you let go of the SHIFT key.

4 Try making a big square, then putting little squares inside it so that they share part of their sides. Overlapping squares can make little squares, too.

5 Make sure you don't miss any squares when you count—you should count them as you draw.

6 Save your file (FILE:SAVE).

7 Write your question at the bottom: "How many squares can you find in this picture?"

8 Print out your game and try it on a friend.

Variations:

- Instead of squares, try making a puzzle with perfect circles or rectangles, or equal-sided triangles. (Holding down the SHIFT key as you draw makes your circles perfect.)

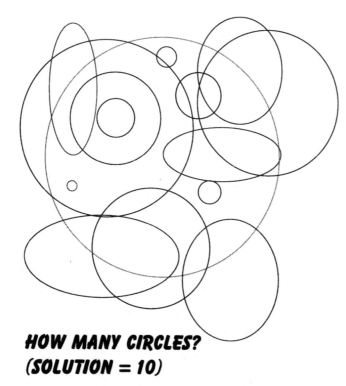

HOW MANY CIRCLES?
(SOLUTION = 10)

- To make the puzzle a little easier, tell the person playing the game how many squares he or she is supposed to find. For example, "Can you find 9 squares in the picture?"

- Try out your game on a couple of friends and see who can find more squares (or circles, or whatever).

Things to WATCH OUT For!

1 Counting rectangles as squares.

2 Not making any perfect squares.

Be sure you are using the drawing tool correctly so that the squares are really square.

A-Maze-Zing
Mazes

22

You've probably already done lots of mazes, but have you ever made one of your own? It can be even trickier than doing them. And you might even find it hard to get through your own maze when you're done.

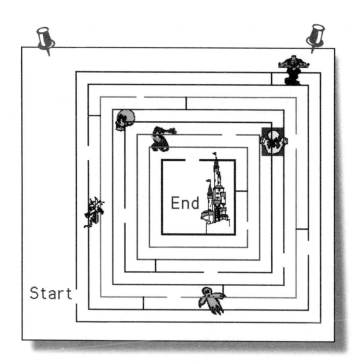

Things You'll Need

paper

What You Do

1 Open your program.

2 Create a new document. (Usually the program does this automatically. If not, FILE:NEW.)

3 Draw the largest square you can make on the screen. Hold down the SHIFT key as you use the rectangle tool to make it a perfect square.

4 About ½ centimeter (¼ inch) inside that square, draw a smaller square. If you make a mistake, go directly to EDIT:UNDO and do it over.

5 Continue drawing as many concentric squares as you can on the screen. (*Concentric* means "one inside the other.")

6 Save your file (FILE:SAVE). (You can use this same drawing of concentric squares to make different mazes, so you might want to add this art to your clip art file.)

7 Using the eraser, erase a section of the biggest square.

8 Type or draw the word "Start" near this break.

9 Use the eraser to erase a part of each square so you can move through all of the squares without crossing a line. There has to be at least one hole in each square so you can get through to the middle. Make sure the holes aren't in the same place on any two squares. Type or draw the word "End" inside the center box.

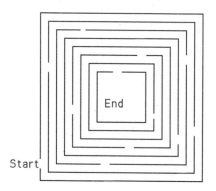

10 Save your changes (FILE:SAVE AS) and print.

11 On your printed copy, use a pencil to trace how you could follow the paths between the squares and through the holes to get to the middle. This is the solution to your maze.

12 Go back to the maze on the computer and erase some different places on the squares.

13 Using the straight line tool, draw some short lines connecting some of the squares. Hold down the SHIFT key when you use the straight line tool to make straight lines.

14 Save your changes (FILE:SAVE) and check your maze. Make sure that your lines block people from going through the new holes all the way to the middle, but don't block the path of your solution. If you can't tell whether that works by looking at your computer screen, save your file again and print the maze out. It's easier to follow on paper, using a pencil.

15 After you check your maze, you may have to erase some of the lines you added so that your solution still works, or put new ones in to prevent people from getting to the middle in a different way.

16 When you're done, save your changes (FILE:SAVE) and print (FILE:PRINT).

17 Before you give your maze to anyone to do, trace your maze again from start to end with a pencil to make sure there is at least one way to get to the end.

Things to WATCH OUT For!

1 Making your maze too easy.

Be sure to set up enough roadblocks and false doors to make the maze confusing.

2 Making your maze too hard.

Be sure that there is a solution!

Variations:

● Change the shape of your maze. Try using a triangle, a robot, a guitar, or some other shape.

● Make more than one entrance to your maze. Which one gets you to the middle?

● Put pictures of different monsters or dinosaurs at the dead ends, some kind of treasure at the end of the maze, and so forth.

What's the Difference?

Finding Changes in Two Drawings

23

In this game, you create drawings that look exactly the same, but actually have several small differences. For example, a flower might have five petals in one drawing but only four in the other.

If you do this by hand, it's hard not to make too many accidental differences, because you have to draw the picture all over again. But on a computer, you can just make little changes to an exact copy.

Make sure to write the number of changes you made somewhere on the page so that the person playing the game will know when to stop looking.

How many differences can you find?

(Six: different roof pattern, doorknob color changes, tree trunk wider in second picture, extra flower in second picture, more birds in second picture, no line for ground in second picture.)

What You Do

1 Open your program.

2 Create a new file. (Usually the program does this automatically. If not, FILE:NEW.)

3 Draw one picture that fills up only half of the screen.

4 Select the picture you have just drawn and copy it (EDIT: COPY).

5 Paste this picture to the right of the original.

6 Save your file (FILE:SAVE).

7 In one of the pictures, make six subtle changes. For example, change the pattern of the roof, or add an extra bird in the sky.

8 Type "Find six differences between these two pictures," either above or below your pictures.

9 Save your changes (FILE:SAVE).

10 Print!

11 Make sure *you* can find the six differences before you give it to someone else to try.

• •

Variation:

● Create the basic drawing yourself, but ask a friend to make the changes. Then you can play this game yourself!

• •

Things to WATCH OUT For !

Not writing down the correct number of differences. When you finish, go through the drawing and make sure that the six differences are really all there and that you can actually see them.

FIND THAT WORD
Word Search Puzzles

24

A word search puzzle is a bunch of letters arranged in boxes that can be read together as words. The letters in the words might read up, down, backward, forward, or diagonally. You are given a list of words that can be found in the puzzle. When you find a word on the list in the puzzle, you draw a line all the way around it.

The instructions are slightly different for a word processor with graphics and for a graphics program, so use the instructions that apply to your software.

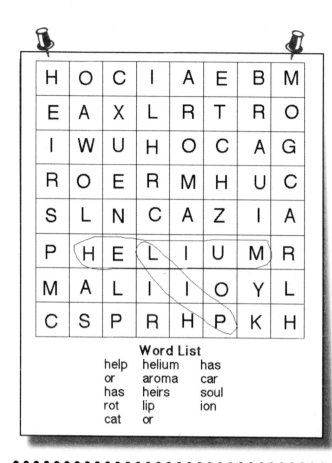

Word List

help	helium	has
or	aroma	car
has	heirs	soul
rot	lip	ion
cat	or	

Things You'll Need

paper

What You Do

Using a graphics program

1 Open your program.

2 Create a new file. (Usually programs do this automatically. If not, FILE:NEW.)

3 Create a grid (many rows of small boxes), using the line tool to draw the lines. To make straight lines, hold down the SHIFT key when you draw.

4 Make as many boxes as you want. The boxes should be large enough to fit a letter in. Try to make all the boxes the same size.

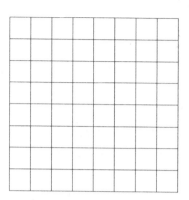

5 Save the grid (FILE:SAVE) before you fill it in so you can make more puzzles later. You may want to add it to your clip art collection (see page 7).

6 Type or draw one capital letter in each square. (In some programs, such as KidPix, you can stamp the letters in with a special stamp tool.)

Make the letters big so that they're easy to see. You can put in letters randomly and look for words yourself, or put a few words in first then fill up the other squares to hide them. Remember, words can go sideways, up or down, backward, and diagonally.

7 Type a list of the words in your puzzle underneath it.

8 Save your file with a new name (FILE:SAVE AS) and print.

What You Do

Using a word processor with graphics

1 Open your program.

2 Create a new file. (Usually programs do this automatically. If not, FILE:NEW.)

3 Create a table, if your program has this feature. (The actual command changes from program to program; usually it's something like Insert: Table, or Table: Insert Table.) Put one row in the table for every line of your word search puzzle, and one column for every letter going across.

4 If you can, format your table with lines around each cell of the table. (Again, the command is different in every program; usually it's something like Table: Borders or Format: Borders and Shading: Grid.) If you can't do this in the program, you can always draw the lines by hand after you print it out.

5 Click in each cell (each box) of your table and type a letter. Instead of clicking, you can also move to the next cell by pressing the TAB key.

Make the letters big so that they're easy

to see. You can put in letters randomly and look for words yourself, or put a few words in first, then fill up the other squares to hide them. Remember, words can go sideways, up or down, backward, and diagonally.

6 Below your puzzle, type a list of the words in it.

7 Save your file and print it out.

Variations:

- You can make it harder by not putting the word list below the puzzle.

- Use family names or friends' names as the puzzle words.

- If you are going on a trip, use names of landmarks, places you are visiting, famous people, and so on.

- Make your own rules for the puzzles! You could only count words that are backward, or words that are diagonal.

- Have someone solve the puzzles on the computer. He or she can use drawing tools (like a pencil tool) to circle words. Print out the solution.

Things to WATCH OUT For!

Not making the squares of the grid large enough.

After drawing a few squares, test to make sure that the letters will fit in them.

INTERNET HUNT
Finding Information on the Internet

25

The Internet has lots of interesting stuff on it, and most of it is free. Sometimes it's hard to know how to find it, though! This game challenges you to look up some facts, like the capital of Slovakia. Have fun finding out about the world and impress your friends with your ability to answer almost any question.

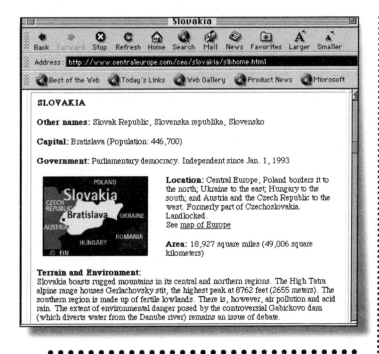

Things You'll Need

Internet access

paper

What You Do

1 Open your Web browser and your word processor.

2 Choose a search engine (usually you can click a "search" button and it will bring up several choices). One good

search engine for kids is Yahooligans (www.yahooligans.com).

3 Search the Internet to find the answer. Here are some searching tips:

- Search for a word or phrase that relates to the question. Phrases should be put in quote marks. The longer the phrase, the more likely you are to find an exact match. For example, for question #1 below, you should search under "United States Secretary of the Interior" (and make sure you type in the quote marks).

- If you don't have an exact phrase, type as many words about the subject as possible. When the words aren't in quotes, the computer will look for Web pages that use all of these words in any order. So for question #4 below, you might type the words *Slovakia*, and *capital*, and *city*. For question #3 you might try *weather*, and *Atlanta*, and *temperature*. There's no exactly right way to do it—just experiment.

4 After you do your search, the search Web page will show you a list of Web pages that it thinks have what you are looking for. The first ones are the most likely to match, so you should try them first. Each description of a page is also a link (usually underlined in blue). That means if you click on it, you will go to that page.

5 Click on the first Web page listed and look at it. If it has what you're looking for, you're done! If the page isn't right, click the Back button in your browser. This will take you back to your list of possible matches, so you can try a different page. Usually a link changes color after you've looked at its page, so you know which ones you've already looked at.

6 Look over the list again and try another page. Be sure to read the description of each page—sometimes you can tell that the next match is wrong just by the description, or you can see a better match further down the list.

7 Sometimes a page might not have what you are looking for, but it might have a link to a page that sounds like what you want. Remember, links are underlined and usually blue. You can click on the link to see that page. If it isn't right either, click the Back button once to get back to the previous page; click twice to get back to your search results.

8 If none of the pages are even close, or you tried all of them, you might have to try doing your search over with different words. For example, if you type a long phrase in quotes and the computer says "no pages match," you need to try again. Maybe you made a spelling mistake (you have to spell things exactly right). Or you can try with a shorter phrase, for example "Secretary of the Interior" instead of "United States Secretary of the Interior."

9 Once you find the answer, type it in your word processor next to its number and go to the next question.

10 Show the same list to a friend and see if he or she can find the answers.

Question List:

1 Who is the United States Secretary of the Interior?

2 Who wrote the palindrome "A man, a plan, a canal: Panama"?

3 What is the temperature right now in Atlanta, Georgia?

4 What is the capital city of the country Slovakia?

5 What is the name of the money used in Poland? How many are equal to one United States dollar (as of today—it changes every day)?

Things to WATCH OUT For!

1 Using search words that are too general.

Sometimes you'll get hundreds of possible sites that fit your search word. Work on narrowing your search by using more specific words or combination of words.

2 Using up too much time. Sometimes a search takes longer than you think, or you just get interested in stuff that's off the subject. Give yourself a time limit before you start searching so that you're not spending a lot of money on the Internet connection.

3 Finding a site that is weird or offensive.

Click the Back button immediately to exit the site.

Variations:

- Have someone make up a list of questions for you to answer. See how fast you can find them.

- Make your own list by exploring the Internet and writing down interesting facts you find. Try looking at the "What's New" and "What's Cool" pages on your Web browser. Make up questions from the facts you found and give the list of questions to friends for their own Internet Hunt. To make it easier, give them some clues with each question.

Section IV

PARTY THINGS

*U*se your computer to make some things for a party! Give your guests a map of how to get to your house, included in an invitation you create. When your guests arrive, have them wear masks you've designed as you send them off on a treasure hunt!

You're Invited!
Making Invitations

26

Nobody will know you're having a party if you don't invite them! You could just tell them or call them up, but it's more fun to give them a real printed invitation, either in person or by mail. And with computers you can make really neat invitations.

IT'S A POOL PARTY
AT JOHN'S!

7:00 P.M.
MAY 27
1200 WASHINGTON ST.

BRING: A TOWEL,

SWIMSUIT, MUSIC.

RSVP: 555-3444

Things You'll Need

paper (maybe something a little fancier than the usual paper in your printer)

crayons, colored pencils, or markers

What You Do

1 Open your program.

2 Create a new file. (Most programs do this automatically. If not, FILE:NEW.)

3 Turn on text centering. The command is different in different programs, but it usually says Alignment or Justification, and you set it to Center. If there's a button, it usually shows several lines that are centered.

4 At the top of the page, in large type, put something to get attention, like "It's a party!" or "Birthday party!"

5 Below that, type your party information: time, date, location, your phone number for replies ("RSVP"), and what you expect people to bring (like bathing suits if it's a swimming party, or pajamas if it's a slumber party). Don't ask your guests to bring presents. They can if they want to, but it's not polite to ask for them. If you *don't* want gifts, then say so on your invitation.

6 Save your file (FILE:SAVE).

7 Format your text. Play around with the size, style, fonts, and text color (if you have a color printer).

8 Add art. If the program allows, you can draw right on the invitation, or you can use clip art from your clip art collection (see page 7).

9 If you want, you can add a border. Either draw lines around the writing, or use a ready-made frame or border from your collection (see page 11).

10 Save your changes (FILE:SAVE).

11 Print! See the special printing ideas below under "Variations."

Variations:

● Print a copy, then cut around it (removing the blank edges) and glue it on top of colored or fancy paper.

● If you can use a photocopy machine, make one original then copy the other invitations from it. If you have a lot of invitations to make, this might be cheaper and faster than printing out many copies from your computer. If you have an older (dot matrix) printer that needs special paper, you might have to photocopy if you want the invitations to be on fancy paper.

● Write your message in different ways: as a rebus (see page 111), or in a secret code (see page 103).

Things to WATCH OUT For!

1 Pictures that are cut off on the sides.

Most printers have a "printable area," which is usually everything a half-inch or more inside the edges of your paper. Any part of your invitation that is outside this area, or is outside the margins, won't be printed.

You can fix this problem by making the margins smaller, or moving words and pictures away from the edge of your paper. Change the margins by going to FILE:PAGE SETUP and change all margins to 0.5 inches. That's usually as small as you can go.

2 Text that is covered by the pictures.

This happens because the words, and each individual picture, are in different layers that can be on top of one another. Usually you want the words on top and the pictures underneath.

Try clicking on the picture so that you see little black squares around its edges. Now move the picture away from the text. You could also put the picture layer behind the text layer by selecting the graphic, then choosing ELEMENT:SEND TO BACK or ARRANGE:SEND TO BACK (in most programs). This will put the picture underneath the words, allowing you to see both.

HOW DO I GET THERE?
Map to a Party

27

Having a party? Give your friends and guests easy directions for finding your home. Once you have a map to your home on the computer, everyone in your family can use it (faxing copies at the last minute to visitors, or inserting them with invitations). Ask for feedback as you work to make sure you haven't left anything out, or someone might get lost!

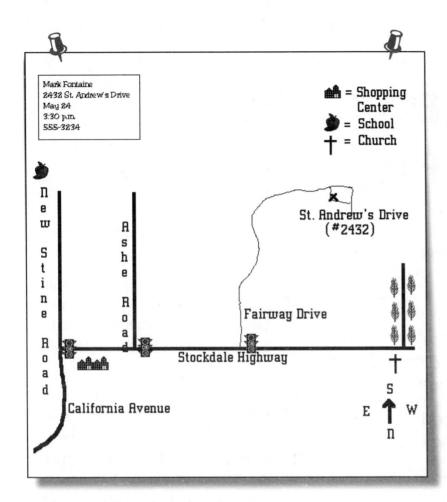

Mark Fontaine
2432 St. Andrew's Drive
May 24
3:30 pm
555-3234

= Shopping
Center

= School

= Church

New Stine Road

Ashe Road

St. Andrew's Drive
(#2432)

Fairway Drive

Stockdale Highway

California Avenue

S
E → W
N

Things You'll Need

paper

any town, city, or state maps you can use as guides

What You Do

1 Open your program.

2 Create a new file. (Usually programs do this automatically. If not, FILE:NEW.)

3 Type your party information at the top: your name, your address, and the date and time of your party. Add your phone number, too, so that if anyone gets lost they can call.

4 Using a printed map as a guide, draw an outline of the streets you need to show. Start from the nearest highway, and make sure you include all of the big streets leading up to your house. You can make a straight line in most graphics programs by holding down the SHIFT key while you draw with the line tool. Make sure you let go of the mouse before you let go of the SHIFT key. If you have trouble clicking on lines, make sure that the tip of the arrow is touching the line.

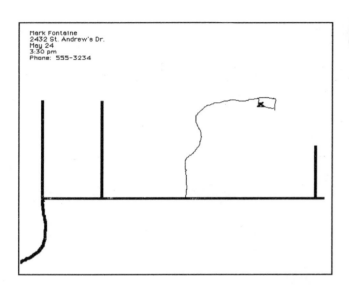

Mark Fontaine
2432 St. Andrew's Dr.
May 24
3:30 pm
Phone: 555-3234

5 Make the lines for important streets thicker. In most graphics programs, there are different boxes you can click on to make a line thicker or thinner. Click on a street you've already drawn, then click the thick line box; or you can click the thick line box before you draw the line. If you make a mistake in drawing a line, erase that line and draw it again. (You can erase by choosing EDIT:UNDO, or clicking on the line and pressing the DELETE key.) This is usually easier than trying to fix a line with a mistake.

6 Save your file (FILE: SAVE), and give it a name with the word "map" in it.

7 Double-check what you have so far. Will there be enough room for all of the streets, blocks, and places you need? Don't try to squeeze things in at the end of the page. The person reading the map will expect these things to be closer together than they really are.

8 Type in the names of the streets. You don't have to list *every* street, just those on which people will travel and some others on either side of those streets so they know what is coming and if they have gone too far. You can hand-draw names with the pencil tool or use a typing tool to type the names. Sometimes you can rotate these words if that makes the map easier to read.

9 Add helpful landmarks to your map: rectangles for houses; lines for railroad tracks; religious symbols for churches, mosques, and synagogues; trees for parks; and so on.

10 You'll need to make a legend for your map. A legend lists any symbols used in your map and shows what they mean (for example ⬡ = stop sign, ⬥ = school, † = church). You can insert symbols like these with a special command in many programs, usually something like INSERT: SYMBOL, or KEY CAPS on a Macintosh computer. Or you can draw your own symbols, or use clip art (see page 7).

11 Mark your home with a big X ("X marks the spot!"). And put the number of your house next to it.

12 Save the changes you've made to your file (FILE:SAVE).

13 Print some copies of what you have so far and ask people to make written corrections and suggestions that you can add to your computer file later. Then test your map by taking it with you while you walk or ride your bike along the streets. It's easy to think you remember how a street goes, but really forget part of it.

14 Make any additional changes, save your file (FILE:SAVE), and print out your finished map.

Things to WATCH OUT for!

1 Running out of space for all of the streets on the map. Check on this early. Otherwise, you may have to start all over!

2 Not leaving enough space to write the names of the streets.

Variations:

● Instead of one map for everybody, you could make a special map for each individual friend, showing how to come directly from their house over to yours.

● You can write out directions in words below your map.

● Map your way to school.

● Map your way to a friend's house.

● Map your way to your grandparents' houses.

MASQUERADE
Party Masks

28

It doesn't have to be Halloween to wear masks! Catwoman wears one every day. It's a silly and fun way to spice up your day.

Of course, the main time when people wear masks, besides Halloween, is for parties such as a costume party or masquerade ball. The word "masquerade" even comes from the French word for mask. Make your next party a masquerade and follow this project to make enough masks for everyone.

Things You'll Need

paper

colored pencils, crayons, markers, glitter, or paints

scissors

string or yarn

single-hole punch

pictures of masks from other countries, to give ideas for masks (optional)

clear contact paper for covering the decorated masks (optional)

What You Do

1 Open your program.

2 Create a new file. (Usually programs automatically do this. If not, FILE:NEW.)

3 Use the straight line tool or the freehand drawing tool to make a mask outline as wide as your screen. Choose one of these shapes, or make your own.

4 Use the circle tool to draw spaces for eyeholes.

5 Draw designs or pictures to decorate your mask. Or draw crazy lines, then fill in open gaps with the fill tool (usually this looks like a spilling paint bucket). Leave lots of blank space for coloring later, or use color on the computer if you have a color printer. If you want, you could look

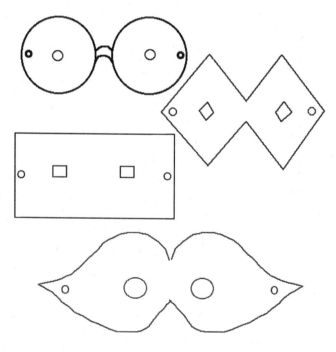

in your local library for books with mask designs from different countries. You could also use clip art (see page 7) to decorate your mask.

6 Save your file (FILE:SAVE).

7 Print a copy (FILE:PRINT).

8 Add any coloring you want to do by hand.

9 (Optional) You can cover the mask with clear contact paper or laminate it, if you want it to last longer and be waterproof.

10 Cut out the eyeholes.

11 Punch a hole on each side of the mask and tie the ends of your string or yarn to it.

12 Put on your mask!

Things to WATCH OUT For!

Making masks too small. Be sure to make your mask as big as possible. It's easier to size them down if you need to later. If the mask is too big or too small, you can fix this. In many programs, you can choose FILE:PAGE SETUP and change the printing size to make the mask bigger or smaller. To make the mask bigger, increase the printing size to a percentage larger than 100%. To make the mask smaller, decrease the printing size to a percentage smaller than 100%.

Variations:

- Make identical masks for your friends to wear.
- Print extra copies of a shape you like and color it different ways.
- Try making a mask that looks silly, like outrageous glasses with crazy eyes.
- Make masks for friends and relatives.
- Design masks based on your favorite action heroes and book characters.

WHERE'S MY PRESENT?
Treasure Hunt

Everyone loves a treasure hunt (even grown-ups!). So next time you have a present to give, make a treasure hunt that leads to the gift.

A treasure hunt is a series of clues. The first clue tells you to go to a certain place to find the next clue. The next clue leads you to more clues, and so on. The final clue says where the present really is.

It's icy in igloos and in here...

Things You'll Need

paper

crayons, colored pencils, or markers

scissors

tape

What You Do

1 Open your program.

2 Create a new document. (Usually the software does this automatically. If not, FILE:NEW.)

3 Type a list of places where you could hide clues. They can be all inside your home, around your yard, or even out in your neighborhood. Just be sure the places are all safe to be wandering around in and are easy enough to get to. This list is for you only—don't show it! Here's an example:

Bathroom

Computer

Backyard

Kitchen

4 Next to each location, type exactly where you will hide the clue.

Bathroom—taped behind the mirror

Computer—in a folder named "party"

Backyard—under the table

Kitchen—inside the freezer

5 Save your file (FILE:SAVE).

6 For each of these places, write a clue that tells where to look next.

For example, the first clue might say:

"Flush! Stop looking at yourself!"

(This tells your friend to go into the bathroom and look in the mirror.)

In the bathroom, taped to the back of the mirror, a note says:

"Okay, now look in the computer under 'DO NOT OPEN'!"

On the computer, in a folder named "DO NOT OPEN," there is a file named "POISON" that says:

Hello, Fred.

A B C D E F G H I J K L M
C D E F G H I J K L M N O

N O P Q R S T U V W X Y Z
P Q R S T U V W X Y Z A B

DCEMACTF—VCDNG!

That's a code in which each letter of the alphabet corresponds to a different letter. When Fred solves it, the line in code reads: "BACKYARD—TABLE!"

Underneath the backyard table, there's a note that says:

"Okay, last clue . . . It's icy in igloos and in here . . ."

If Fred looks inside the kitchen freezer, he will find his present.

7 Format your clues in fun, bold, and large fonts to type them. Pictures are fun, too. You could even have a clue with no words, just pictures! Leave enough space above and below each clue so that you can cut them apart.

8 Save your changes (FILE:SAVE).

9 Print your clues and use the crayons, colored pencils, or markers to decorate them.

10 Cut the clues apart so that each clue is on its own piece of paper.

11 Hide the clues in their proper places according to your list. Fold the papers and use the tape to stick them to places like the back of the mirror and the underside of the table.

12 Ask a friend to try the hunt to make sure it isn't too hard and that you haven't left any clues out. Remember, you know all the answers—it's harder for everybody else. Make sure that someone reading this for the first time will get it. Clues should be tricky but not impossible.

Variation:

● You can make a treasure hunt with the clues in secret codes (see page 103) to make the game harder.

Things to WATCH OUT For!

1 Clues that are too hard.

2 Clues that disappear.
Make some extra copies just in case, and check to see that all the clues are still there when the game is about to begin.

3 Clues that get found too early.
Wait until just before the event to put them out.

4 Clues that seem endless.
Don't make too many clues, or people will get bored and annoyed. Three or four is a good number.

Section V

SECRET CODES

Armies and spies have used secret codes for hundreds of years. They are a great way to share secrets with your closest friends, and they're also fun to create and figure out (or "crack"), just like any puzzle.

Now all you super sleuths and spy wannabes can make your own codes. The specifics of each type of code are different, but all of them work in the same general way. Before you try some different codes, here is the general way to set up a code and the "key" that will help you solve it.

General Code Instructions (Making a Codekey)

1 Type out all of the letters of the alphabet, pressing the TAB key after each one. You will need to do this on two or three lines. When you get near the end of a line, press the RETURN (or ENTER) key three times to make room for your code and a space between lines.

2 When you're done, save this as a file named "codekey." This will be the starting point for most of your codes. Every time you want to make a new code, open this file and make a copy of it (FILE:SAVE AS) with a different name.

3 In your new copy, put the code for each letter right underneath the letter. For example, if the code for "A" is "1," type a 1 directly underneath the A. You will need to tab after each code, just like you did with the letters. (Using the TAB key instead of the space bar will make sure that the code and the letter line up.) Format your code as bold so it looks different from your letters.

4 Save your file (FILE:SAVE). This is called the *key* to your code because it helps you unlock the coded message.

A Codekey

A	B	C	D	E	F
1	2	3	4	5	6

G	H	I	J	K	L
7	8	9	10	11	12

M	N	O	P	Q	R	S
13	14	15	16	17	18	19

T	U	V	W	X	Y	Z
20	21	22	23	24	25	26

For example, if your message had a "5" in it, you would look on this key and see that 5 means "E."

5 Double-check your code to make sure that each code letter or picture only stands for one real letter. If "7" is both "B" and "R," your friend won't know which letter it means.

6 Open a new file (FILE:NEW) and write a message using your code. It's usually easier to write your message normally first, then write it in code right below. Delete the uncoded words when you're done.

H-E-L-L-O

8-5-12-12-15

With numbered codes, it helps to mark spaces between individual characters with a hyphen (-) so you know where one number ends and the next one begins.

7 After you write your message, decode it yourself to make sure it works before you send it.

8 Give your coded message and its key to a friend. These basic steps are the same for all of the codes that follow.

SCRAMBLED LETTERS
Alphabet Code

30

One of the simplest codes to make, and one of the hardest to read, is the scrambled alphabet code, where you switch each letter with a different letter. To decipher it, you simply replace each letter with its equivalent, using your codekey.

ZDBX BNA JPO LPVMR BGXAN UIDPPW?

What are you doing after school?

• •

Things You'll Need   paper

• •

What You Do

1 Open your program.

2 Open your codekey template (see page 104) and make a copy (FILE:SAVE AS). Give it a different name.

3 Print a copy of the blank key (it just has the letters A through Z on it).

4 Click below the "A" and type a different letter. Whichever letter you use, cross it off on your printout so you don't use it twice accidentally.

5 Press TAB so you're under the "B." Type a letter for its code, and cross that letter off on your printout. Repeat with all the letters until you have finished the entire alphabet.

A	B	C	D	E	F	G	H	I	J	K	L	M
B	K	I	L	A	G	R	D	V	C	E	W	Y

N	O	P	Q	R	S	T	U	V	W	X	Y	Z
M	P	S	F	N	U	X	O	H	Z	T	J	Q

6 Now you have a code and a key to solve it. Save your file (FILE:SAVE).

7 After the last letter of your code, press the RETURN key five times, then begin writing your message.

First type what you want to say, then translate that message into code. Use a space to separate words. When you are done, erase the original message, leaving only the code.

8 After you write your message in code, decode it yourself to make sure it works!

9 Save your changes (FILE:SAVE), and print both the message and codekey. Give them to your friends and see if they can figure it out.

Variations:

- Have a birthday party with a spy theme and use a secret code for the invitations.

- Have a treasure hunt (see page 99) using secret codes for the clues.

Things to WATCH OUT for!

Don't write too much. Remember, whoever reads your message will have to spend some time figuring out each letter.

PICTURE THIS
Using Pictures for Letters

Before alphabets were invented, the first form of writing used little pictures to explain things. Gradually, people used the same pictures to mean the same things. This is how the Egyptians wrote. They called it "hieroglyphics." Chinese characters are distant descendants of these; there is no standard alphabet, and each word has its own picture.

In those languages, the pictures are meant to look like what they mean. But since we are making a secret code, we'll make a picture for each letter of the alphabet, and make sure that the picture doesn't give away which letter it is.

31

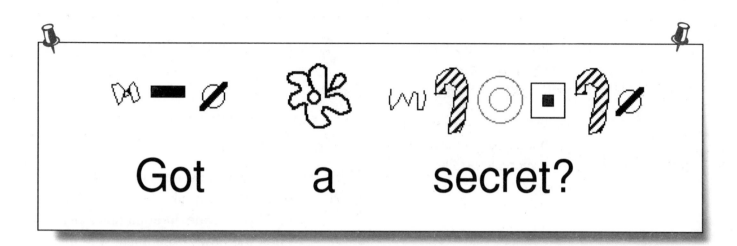

Got a secret?

Things You'll Need   paper

What You Do

1 Open your codekey template file (see page 104). Make a copy (FILE:SAVE AS) and give it a different name.

2 Put a picture below each letter in your codekey file. How you do this depends on your software.

    a) If you have a graphics program with preset "stamps" (such as KidPix or KidWorks)

        Using the stamps, stamp a picture below each letter.

(You can't read this.)

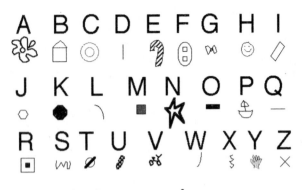

(Funny Money)

b) If you have a graphics program without "stamps"

Draw small pictures below each letter, or use pictures from your clip art file (page 7).

3 Save your file (FILE:SAVE).

4 Write your message first, then translate it into code.

5 After you write your message in code, decode it yourself to make sure it works!

6 Save your changes (FILE:SAVE), and print your codekey and message.

Variation:

● You could use special characters on your keyboard, like %, &, and * to build your code, in addition to pictures you draw. Experiment with the OPTION and ALT keys, or use the tools for special characters (KeyCaps on the Macintosh, Character Map in Windows 95, or Insert: Symbol in many word processors) to find more unusual characters.

Things to WATCH OUT For!

1 Writing too much.
Remember it will take a while to translate your message.

2 Using the same picture for two different letters.
Make sure each picture or symbol is only used for one letter, and that no two pictures look a lot like each other.

REBUSES
Combining Pictures and Letters

32

A rebus is a puzzle that uses a combination of pictures and letters to represent words. You look at each picture and try to figure out what word it means. Then you add and subtract letters to get your message.

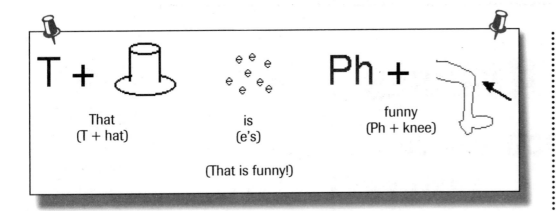

That
(T + hat)

is
(e's)

funny
(Ph + knee)

(That is funny!)

Things You'll Need

paper

What You Do

1 Open your program.

2 Create a new file. (Usually the program does this automatically. If not, FILE:NEW.)

3 Think of a simple sentence you could write as a rebus.

4 Draw the pictures for your rebus. Either use a drawing tool or cut and paste something from your clip art collection (see page 7.)

5 Use a plus sign or a minus sign to add or subtract letters, if you need to. For example, for "That" you could write T + 🎩.

6 Here are a few suggestions to help you write your codes:

- water = H_2O
- and = N or &

- to make something plural, just draw several of them
- try thinking about homonyms (words that are spelled differently but sound the same), such as son = sun, I = eye, to = too = two

7 Sometimes you might write the entire word if you're really stuck.

8 When you're finished, save your file (FILE:SAVE), and print a copy.

Variation:

- Use rebuses for party invitations, birthday cards, private notes, or postcards.

Things to WATCH OUT For! Trying to make a rebus out of a sentence that's too difficult. If you are stuck on one word, you can get away with just writing it out, but if you keep getting stuck, it's time to come up with an easier sentence.

SECRET SYMBOLS
Using Symbols for Letters

33

Most word processors have a font that writes nonsense characters, or little pictures, or special symbols (like letters from other alphabets and scientific symbols).

This is an unusual code because you don't need a key—all you have to do is change the font back to a normal font, like Times New Roman or Courier, to be able to read it.

The only trick is that you need to give the person you are writing to a computer file instead of a printout, because there's no way to change the font on a piece of paper.

(I'M HUNGRY)

4 When you have completed your message, highlight the text, then choose a font (FORMAT:FONT) like "Symbol," "Zapf Dingbats," or "Wing Dings," that automatically puts the message into code.

5 Save your file (FILE:SAVE).

6 Send your message to your friend as a computer file. You can send a copy on a disk or attach it as a file to E-mail.

7 Tell your friend to open the file, then change the font to a regular font such as Times New Roman or Courier.

Things You'll Need
paper

What You Do

1 Open your program.

2 Create a new file. (Usually programs do this automatically. If not, FILE:NEW.)

3 Type in your message using the regular alphabet. Double-check it for spelling (you could use your Spell Checker).

Variations:

● Try different fonts. Look through the list of fonts in your computer to see what they look like. Most will just print out the words in different style letters, but that's interesting, too.

● Try giving your friend just a printout of your message and see if he or she can crack the code.

COUNT ON THIS
Number Code

34

This code uses numbers to represent letters.

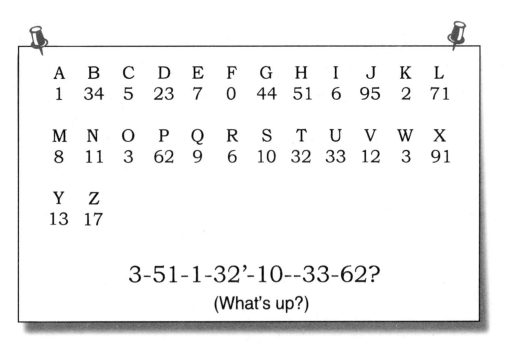

A	B	C	D	E	F	G	H	I	J	K	L
1	34	5	23	7	0	44	51	6	95	2	71

M	N	O	P	Q	R	S	T	U	V	W	X
8	11	3	62	9	6	10	32	33	12	3	91

Y	Z
13	17

3-51-1-32'-10--33-62?

(What's up?)

Things You'll Need   paper

What You Do

1 Open your program.

2 Open your codekey template (see page 104) and make a copy (FILE:SAVE AS). Give it a different name.

3 Use numbers to make your code. Some letters may have two-digit numbers (like 23) or three-digit numbers (like 743). Make sure you don't use the same number for two different letters!

A	B	C	D	E	F	G	H	I	J	K	L	M
7	11	8	2	99	21	0	6	75	82	3	42	1

N	O	P	Q	R	S	T	U	V	W	X	Y	Z
47	20	83	4	50	31	63	5	25	72	9	10	55

4 Save your file (FILE:SAVE).

5 Write your message, then translate it into code. Put a dash after each letter, and two dashes between words.

72-6-7-63 -- 2-75-2 -- 10-20-5 --
11-50-75-47-0 -- 21-20-50 --
42-5-47-8-6?

(WHAT DID YOU BRING
FOR LUNCH?)

6 After you write your message in code, erase the original message.

Make sure to decode the message yourself to see that it works!

7 Save your changes (FILE:SAVE), and print.

Variations:

● Instead of putting two dashes between words, you could just put one dash. This would make it more difficult, because your friend has to figure out where one word stops and the next one begins.

● To make it much harder, give the message to your friend *without* the codekey, or give the key for only a few letters.

Things to WATCH OUT For !

Writing too much. Remember that the person who reads your letter will have to translate every single letter.

Index